MY LIFE BEHIND BARS

A BARTENDER'S GUIDE: RULES, RECIPES AND ONE-LINERS

Just for laughs!

Jim Jung

10.2-02

Second Edition, Revised

Allen Publishing

MY LIFE BEHIND BARS

A BARTENDER'S GUIDE: RULES, RECIPES AND ONE-LINERS

By Jim Jung

Published by:

ALLEN PUBLISHING
Post Office Box 479
Kapaau, Hawaii 96755 U.S.A.

Copyright © 2000 and 2001
By Jim Jung
First Printing 2000
Second Printing 2001, revised

Printed in the United States of America

Library of Congress Control Number: 2001 129064
Title: My Life Behind Bars
Author: Jim Jung

ISBN 0-9708716-1-9 Hardcover
ISBN 0-9708716-2-7 Paperback

CONTENTS

ABOUT THE AUTHOR

Jim Jung was raised on a ranch in Colorado. He was left at the rodeo when he was four, so he knows something about cowboys and clowns.

He held a variety of jobs before spending three years in the U.S. Navy and one year with the U. S. Marine Corps. He was decorated for bravery during Operation Dewey Canyon.

He attended the University of Colorado and earned a B.S. in Journalism. He worked for newspapers in Colorado before leaving during the blizzard of '74 and ensuing fuel crisis. He moved to the one place in the United States where you can live the year around and not freeze to death: Hawaii.

He took up beach combing and lived off the land until he ran out of money. Then he started a newspaper in a small town and sold advertising and printed the news. After two years of that it became more work than money. He put the paper to bed and became a little known, little understood resort bartender.

He considers bartending to be the second best job he has ever had. He was paid to sleep in a hospital.

He is a man of extremes living on the northern tip of the U.S.A.'s most southern island. He drives the biggest car and rides the smallest motorcycle. He lives with his wife and daughter on a hill across from a hardware store and not that far from where they feed the old people for free. What a place to be.

ACKNOWLEDGMENT

I would like to thank the lovely Kathleen Allen for threatening to publish my letters if I did not write a book.

I would like to thank Walter M. Shields for explaining to me how the human is basically lazy and will do nothing if not prodded. I would like to thank his wife Jeanna Shields.

I would like to thank William P. Sloan for taking over the manuscript when it became more than jokes.

I would like to thank Catherine Tarleton and my wife Clara Jung for their work on proofreading.

I would like to thank Daniel K. Marcom and Lester S. Yagi for their computer kokua.

I would like to thank Dan Poynter for pointing the way.

I would like to thank William Kling for everything.

WARNING-DISCLAIMER

This book is a tongue-in-cheek look at bartending. It is sold with the understanding that the publisher and author are not engaged in rendering legal, accounting or other professional services. If legal or other expert assistance is required, the services of a competent professional should be sought.

It is not the purpose of this manual to reprint all the information that is otherwise available to the author and/or publisher, but to complement other texts. You are urged to read all the available material, and learn as much as possible about bartending.

Bartending is a craft. Anyone who decides to engage in it must expect late hours and strange people, a lot of lifting and a lot of standing. For many people bartending is a lucrative enterprise, and they have built solid, growing, rewarding relationships with people they may not have otherwise met.

Every effort has been made to make this book as complete and as accurate as possible. However, there may be mistakes both typographical and in content. Therefore, this text should be used only as a general guide and not as the ultimate source of information concerning bartending. Furthermore, this book contains information on bartending only up to the printing date.

The purpose of this book is to educate and entertain. The author and Allen Publishing shall have neither liability nor responsibility to any person or entity with respect to any loss or damage caused, or alleged to be caused, directly or indirectly by the information contained in this book.

If something makes you laugh pass it on. If something offends you keep it to yourself.

MOTHER

This book is a guide for making drinks and riding motorcycles. It is a work of fiction. All the characters, other than the well known historical figures, referred to in this novel, are fictional, and the product of the author's imagination.

"Before you begin your adult life you should spend one night in jail and one week as a bartender."   Anon

THE RULES OF BARTENDING

The First Rule of Bartending is: DESTROY THE EVIDENCE If a person hands a drink back and says, "This tastes like Fresno on a warm day," take it and pour it down the drain and turn the water on. Throw it in the sink. Get rid of it, so there is nothing left to argue about. If the beer is warm, dump it. If there is ice in the Pina Colada, dump it. If the soda is flat, dump it.

Don't taste it; waste it. Throw it away and say, "What else would you like? Your satisfaction is important to me." The customer is always the customer.

If they say, "I want a better Pina Colada" or whatever they had, tell them the truth. "You don't like the way I make them. Please, have something else." They will try something else, hopefully vodka and tonic or something simple like a beer, and you can make them happy. It is not your fault. You cannot please every palate with the same recipe no more than you can please every id with the same line. I know you make the best drinks in the world. You have to make the best drinks in the world, because you are in competition with me.

If someone has a favorite drink from a hometown bar, they are not going to find it on vacation. They will ask for drinks you have never heard of. Never tell them, "No." The best way, is to say, "Oh, I don't have the ingredients for that." If they can't remember what's in it, don't waste your time trying. Make them something. If it comes back, start at the top.

The Second Rule of Bartending is: BE NICE TO THE COOK You are going to get hungry during your shift and you want the cook to stop what she is doing and make you food. A good relationship with the cook makes the difference between staying on the job or being parked on the john. If the cook needs a pat on the back, a shoulder to cry on or help reaching something on a high shelf, you help. If the cook needs a ride home, a favor, or a hug, you help. You cannot be too nice to the cook. Praise her every chance you get. Tell her what an asset she is to the operation, and how you love her cooking. I tell mine, "Marilyn, you are the reason I come to work."

The Third Rule of Bartending is: BE CAREFUL You never know with whom you are dealing. The only thing you can be sure of in this life, is that nothing is as it first appears. Angels and house detectives come in disguise. Do not confide in strangers. No matter what you say there will be somebody who takes it too seriously.

One afternoon I was cutting up with a bunch of golfers. They had played a good round, and the beer was flowing. They were young, wealthy and healthy. An old guy pushed his way between them and started giving me gas about the sandwich shop being closed. I explained when they run out of food, or customers, they go home. He was not amused, and left in a sour mood. The men around the bar asked, "Why didn't you tell that old guy to take a hike?"

I reminded them of the third rule. (Be careful.) The next evening, at a cocktail party on the lawn, Mr. Meyer introduced me to the new owner. It was the old guy.

I served a red-haired lady a drink and casually asked, "Did you hear about Reagan's new book? *They Tell Me I Was President.*"

She frowned and asked, "Who do I look like?"

" I don't know."

"I am Nancy Reagan's sister."

During the O.J. Simpson trial I asked a customer, "Did you hear O.J. came up with the perfect alibi? He was at a Denny's waiting for service."

He said, "That hits a little close to home. Denny's is one of our companies."

The Garden Club Of America was here. They were good fun, telling jokes and laughing at the bar after their meetings. One asked for a one-liner for the annual report. I said, "You can lead a horticulture, but you can't make her think." You could hear the jaws drop.

After telling some aborigine jokes to a woman from Australia, she turned in a complaint. How did I know she chaired the endowment for the native peoples?

I was telling blind people jokes to a guy. He stopped the routine by saying, "I am an eye surgeon."

I asked a Senator if he'd heard about the kid who goes into a pharmacy and asks for some condoms. He tells the pharmacist, "My girlfriend is going to screw my brains out. Tonight is the night, and I have been waiting on this."

The pharmacist says, "Well, we have a three-pack, a six-pack or a year's supply for a married couple: a dozen."

The boy says, "I will take the six-pack. I will use them all tonight."

He makes his purchase and goes over to his girlfriend's house for dinner. At the table they say grace. After the prayer the kid keeps his head bowed. The girl leans over and says, "You never told me you were so deeply religious."

The young man looks up and says, "You never told me your father was a pharmacist."

The senator looks at me puzzled, and says, "I have four daughters."

Some people pack 12 bags and don't include their sense of humor. Nothing makes you lose your sense of humor like someone asking where it is.

The walls have ears, Big Brother is watching, and be nice to everybody. You never know who your next boss will be.

The Fourth Rule of Bartending is: NEVER GO ANYWHERE EMPTY HANDED If you don't carry the bar the bar carries you. If you take out the trash, come back with a bucket of ice. If you bus the dishes, come back with a box of napkins. If you go to lunch, come back with office supplies. If you take out the dirty linens, come back with a case of beer. Before you leave the bar take a look around and see what needs to go with you.

MINORS

It's a giggle of girls, a gaggle of boys, but an ingratitude of children. Children are like motorcycles. We give them the best and still they go wrong. Your children are like your stomach. They do not need everything you can afford to give them. You can only enjoy your children as long as they are on your side. Rich people's kids put more demands on a society than poor people's kids. There is nothing for them to do at the resort. They resort to vandalism, after the third day, for entertainment. They break into the bar and steal the booze. They break eggs on the rock walls in the sun. They string firecrackers down the halls and light them in the middle of the night. We don't serve minors. They don't tip.

The drinking age in Hawaii was 18. Then it changed to 19 years old. Then the state fell victim to the Federal Government's blackmail legislation and raised the drinking age to 21, to save five million dollars in highway funds. They took the parties out of the bars and put them in the cars. Kids are going to drink under age. Kids are going to buy drinks under age. They will lie to you, give you the biggest bunch of back talk, show a false ID, and cry "Mommy".

Asking for an ID is an unpleasant part of the job. Still, what is just a drink to them are a license and a livelihood for you. Something you have to do. If a kid is 21, and has an ID, he will show it. If they are underage, they want you to call the front desk, or believe they left it in their room.

"I'll wait while you go get it."

"Well I am in my swimming suit. There is no place to carry it."

"You can put it somewhere. It won't melt. Always carry it with you. Make it easy on your next of kin to identify your remains, should you drown. Always carry identification. If there is any trouble and the cops come, you can show them you have a name and an address. That means you have people that will come looking for you, should you disappear.

"If the liquor inspector walks up and wants to see your ID, we can't call the desk, or go to your room. He won't believe your mother. Either you produce an ID that proves you are 21, or we go to Hilo and post a $500 fine, each. I will give you a little hassle. He will give us a big hassle. Some ID's I can accept; some I can't. I want a driver's license, with a picture, and you better be facing front in the mug shot. If you give me an ID that is altered I am to confiscate it and call the police."

The Liquor Commissioner, on this island, sends minors around to stores and bars to buy cigarettes and beer, wine or whiskey. Since everybody knows he does it, the outlets cannot cry, "Entrapment." The agents watch the transaction and if a minor is served, they step in and make a big scene. A fine is levied on the server up to a $1000, and the outlet is fined up to $5000. If you're in doubt as to someone's age, ask. If you think you can get by with it, look around to see whom the witnesses are. Remember there's an inspector behind every tree. Any stranger watching can be a house detective.

Hopefully, minors refused service, will walk away and you won't see them again. Sometimes they return with proof of age and then stiff you every day after for embarrassing them. If someone doing their job is going to embarrass them, they are going to have a tough time in life. Sometimes one is of age and the other isn't.

I carded a man who was of age. His girlfriend didn't have any ID. He was trying to use her prescription for birth control pills as proof of age. I am not here to argue, and called the beverage manager. He listened to the argument and said, "I'm sorry. I have a 16-year-old daughter who has a prescription for birth control pills to control her periods. We can't accept that as proof of age."

"You're sorry all right! You've been sorry since you were born!" scorned the customer.

This was uncalled-for and I was ready to park a rum bottle behind the customer's left ear, for insulting the boss. Do not apologize for things over which you have no control. It makes you weak.

The assistant manager of the hotel walked up and intervened. He leaned between the couple and whispered to the gentleman, "Why don't you and her get the fuck out of here. I have called the police and security is on the way." They split.

One afternoon when it was slow, a tow-headed Texas kid walked up and asked for a beer. I said, "I can't serve you. What are you 15?"

He said, "Don't give me no shit. Give me a Coors."

I opened the cooler, handed him the beer, and replied, "It's all in how you ask."

A lovely young lady ordered a Mai Tai. She stood out among all the bikinis because she was wearing a dress. She was mesmerizing. I made the drink and asked, "Are you 21?"

She said, "No" and stood up.

I handed her the drink, and said, "Here is your reward for being honest."

Girls, if you are under age and want a drink, wear a wedding ring. You can buy a band with a cubic zirconia for a little money. Any bartender seeing it won't care how old you are. If you are married, you need a drink.

Guys be cool. Don't linger on the stool. Stand up straight, look the bartender in the eye and order, between two customers, when he is busy. Then go. Out of sight is out of mind. Don't sit at the bar and try and fit in. You won't.

Kids surround the beach bar. It is the source for sodas, smoothies, slushes, shakes and whatever else they can dream up. You can serve them, but then they have to hit the road. This is a recent change. The policy is revised with each owner. Thirty years ago kids could sit at the bar. The guests would drop off their children on a stool and say, "See you in two weeks" and meant it. We would have those kids all day long, sitting at the bar. It was free baby-sitting. If you told them they couldn't sit at the bar you would have a manager on you like white on rice.

Comes a new owner with a new rule. Now kids can only sit at the bar if their parents are with them. No kids at the bar if live music is being played. Any change brings out the reactionary dogs. "My kid used to sit at this bar without me."

"Well not any more."

"What are we supposed to do then?"

"Hire a baby-sitter?"

"How do you like that? The prices go up and the service goes down. This is the last time we come here."

After 10 years of getting them conditioned to this, we are sold again. This owner has a different rule. Now it's no kids at the bar any time ever. These reactionary dogs are parents who used to sit at the bar, and want their kids to share the experience. We tell them all day, every day, no minors at the bar. They use every means to circumvent this. They have their children stand. They make two rows of stools and sit the kids in the back. They have the small ones on their lap. They move the bar stools into the restaurant so the kids can sit high at the table, but they don't bring the stools back. They defy you and let them sit there anyway. Then the others come over and ask, "Why the double standard? How come their kids can sit at the bar and mine can't?"

I tell them all. "We may look like the Old West, but we have rules. Kids can't sit at the bar. Do you take your kids to bars where you live? Since we like where we live and work, we must comply with the local laws." They seem to think the sign that says "No Minors" is for someone else's kids.

The kids usually leave after being served, if you tell them future service will be denied and they will be sold as slaves. And, sometimes you will be surprised. A sudden rain scattered the sunbathers. A gentleman placed a baby, in a bassinet, on the bar. I told him, "Sir, no kids at the bar."

He turned to his wife, and said, "You hear that?" He handed her the basket and she ran to the room. He took out a cigar, smiled at me and said, "Thanks."

I would rather have a world with kids, than without them. Two 10-year-old girls stopped to use the phone. While one was on it, the other said, "Oh no, here they come." I looked and saw two little boys heading our way.

As they approached, one said, "Hey girls I'm sorry about what I said. I didn't mean it." They started walking away. The lad continued, "Just send me a picture of you. That's all I want is a picture." He shouted after them, "With your clothes off!"

The thing about standing 25 years in one place is you see kids grow up and have kids of their own. Some kids are terrors and a problem until they go away from home and somebody tough has them for breakfast. They come back as perfect ladies and gentlemen. It is amazing. Teenagers are the reason mothers understand why some animals eat their young.

I told Valerie, "God is a woman. Every night I ask her for help. I call her Rhonda."

She blew cigarette smoke and glared, "If God was a woman, there would be an easier way to have children."

RECIPES

Everything in life can be equated to pizza.

The better the ingredients, the better the overall product. If you short yourself going in, you will be short coming out. That is the way it equates.

To make the best drinks, use the best ingredients. Find the freshest, finest foods and use premium brands. Don't make a drink that is too strong. You can kill people with kindness. Don't make a drink that is too weak. You want the customer to perceive value. If capital has no return, capital goes elsewhere. The idea is to make a perfect drink and sell them two. The bigger the bottom-line the bigger the tip for you. You must think of yourself as a gratuity generator.

Speed will come after you make a few drinks. There are hundreds of drinks. You will have to make twelve. You must be able to make those twelve at the rate of ten a minute for eight hours. Anybody can be a bartender. Not everybody can run a fast bar. When the crowd is waiting and the pressure is on, every drink gets six seconds.

The fastest way to make drinks is to use equal parts and half parts. For the recipes below, the ingredients are measured in shots (1-1/4 oz.) and 1/2 shots (3/4 oz.). Measure every ingredient every time. Use the jigger for booze, juice, milk, syrup, and rinse it often.

For highballs the ice is put in the glass first. Then the liquor and mix. The theory is it stirs itself as you pour.

For blended drinks, the liquid and fruit go in first, then the ice. You must have at least one-half cup of liquid in the pitcher to break the ice. Otherwise you will break your blender. Cover the blades with liquid, so the top of the nut is showing, throw in a scoop and half of ice, and run it until it sounds like it is wasting its time, and it will fill one glass. Find the line on the pitcher for two drinks. Use three scoops of ice and fill two glasses. Fill the blender pitcher half full of mix and top it with ice and you will make three glasses. Don't come up short, and don't throw any away. You want your guests to be impressed with a perfect glassful every time.

You cannot blend diet sodas. You must have real sugar or animal fat (milk) to hold things in suspension. With diet sodas you get ice and liquid and a big mess on your bar.

Beware of cordials and some after-dinner drinks like Campari and Club Soda. The ice goes in first, then the mix and then the liquor. If you try and pour it like a regular drink, the red stuff lays on the bottom and no amount of poking with a stir stick can get it mixed. You have to box it (pour from glass to glass) to get it to come together...not professional.

For sparkling wines with fruit juices, pour carbonation on top of the juice or you will have bubbles on the bar.

When using frozen concentrated fruit juices mix them double strength. If the directions on the can read three-to-one, make it one and one-half to one. When you mix it with alcohol and pour it on the rocks, or blend it with ice, the added water makes it taste just right and not watered down.

Some drinks are served neat (no ice). Some are served up (chilled no ice). Some are served on ice (rocks). Some are mist (shaved ice). All can be made any way the customer wants. You don't make a dime until you push something across the bar.

Words in all caps are the names of drinks. Words that are capitalized are items found at the liquor store. The items in lower case are food items. Words without a number, or a direction, in front of them mean one-shot (1-1/4 oz.).

ABOMINABLE SNOWMAN Vodka, 1/2 White Creme de Menthe.

THE ALAMO Southern Comfort, fill with grapefruit juice.

ALEXANDER Brandy, milk, 1/2 Dark Creme de Cacao.

AMBROSIA COCKTAIL 1/2 Brandy, dash Cointreau, fill with Champagne.

AMERICANO Campari, Sweet Vermouth, fill with Club Soda.

ANGELS TIP Dark Creme de Cacao, 1/2 milk, float milk off back of bar spoon.

APRICOT SOUR Apricot Brandy, lemon juice, simple syrup.

B-52 Bailey's Irish Cream, Amaretto, Grand Marnier.

BACARDI COCKTAIL Light Rum, lemon juice, simple syrup, dash Grenadine.

BANANA DAIQUIRI Light Rum, lemon juice, simple syrup, 1/2 fresh banana.

BANSHEE COCKTAIL Creme de Banana, 1/2 White Creme de Cacao, milk.

BENEDICTINE & BRANDY Benedictine, float Brandy.

BETWEEN THE SHEETS Creme de Banana, 1/2 Creme de Cacao, milk.

BLACK RUSSIAN Vodka, 1/2 Kahlua.

BLACK VELVET Cointreau, Creme de Cacao, 2 milk.

BLOODY BULL Vodka, 2-consommé soup, 2 Mr. & Mrs. T Bloody Mary mix.

BLOODY MARY Vodka, Rose's Lime Juice, dash Tabasco, dash Worcestershire Sauce, dash Angostura Bitters, dash horseradish, fill with Mr. and Mrs. T Blood Mary mix, shake pepper.

BLOOMER DROPPER Scotch, Galliano, dash Cointreau.

BLUE HAWAII Vodka, lemon juice, simple syrup, pineapple juice, Blue Curacao.

BLUE TAIL FLY Blue Curacao, White Creme de Cacao, 2 milk.

BLUE VELVET Vodka, Kahlua, milk.

BOBBY BURNS Scotch, Sweet Vermouth, dash Benedictine.

BOILER MAKER Jack Daniel's, Beer.

BRANDY ICE Brandy, 2 scoops vanilla ice cream.

BRAVE BULL Tequila, 1/2 Kahlua.

BRONX COCKTAIL Gin, 1/2 Dry Vermouth, 1/2 Sweet
Vermouth, fill with orange juice.

BRUNETTE Bourbon, 1/2 Kahlua, fill with milk.

BUFFALO'S MILK Vodka, Bailey's Irish Cream, Kahlua, 1/2
fresh banana, milk.

BULL SHOT Vodka, 1/2 Rose's Lime Juice, dash Tabasco, dash
Worcestershire Sauce, dash Angostura Bitters, dash horseradish,
fill with consommé soup.

CAMPARI COCKTAIL Campari, Gin, Sweet Vermouth.

CANADIAN CARIBOU Canadian Whiskey, orange juice, apple
cider, lemon juice, 1/2 Grenadine.

CAPE COD Vodka, fill with cranberry juice.

CHAMPAGNE COCKTAIL Put a few drops of Angostura bitters
on a sugar cube, drop in a glass, fill with Champagne.

CHI CHI Vodka, coconut syrup, crushed pineapple, milk.

CHERRY BLOSSOM Sloe Gin, orange juice, 1/2 lemon juice,
dash cherry juice.

CHICAGO COCKTAIL Brandy, 1/2 Orange Curacao, dash
Angostura Bitters.

CLOVER CLUB COCKTAIL Gin, lemon juice, 1/2 Grenadine.

CLOVER LEAF Gin, 1/2 lemon juice, 1/2 Grenadine, egg white.

COCONUT WILLIE 2 Vodka, coconut syrup, milk, crushed
pineapple.

COLLINS Collins mix is double strength lemonade. Mix an equal amount of simple syrup, lemon juice and 2 parts water. Use a shot of your base liquor and fill the glass with half Collins mix and half club soda. Vodka, Gin (Tom), Rum, Brandy, Bourbon (John).

CONTINENTAL Brandy, 1/2 Galliano, 1/2 White Creme de Menthe.

COSMOPOLITAN Vodka, Triple Sec, fill with cranberry juice.

CREAM PUFF Rum, milk, 1/2 simple syrup, fill with club soda.

CREME DE MENTHE FRAPPE Pour Green Creme de Menthe over crushed ice.

CRICKET Brandy, Green Creme de Menthe, 2 milk.

CUBA LIBRA Rum, fill with Coca Cola, squeeze lime.

DAIQUIRI Rum, lemon juice, simple syrup.

DIXIE COOLER Southern Comfort, lemon juice, Grenadine.

DOUBLE SUNDOWNER Scotch, Coca-Cola.

DUBONNET COCKTAIL Dubonnet, Gin.

FIFTH AVENUE Dark Creme de Cacao, Apricot Brandy, milk.

FLAMINGO Gin, 1/2 Apricot Brandy, orange juice, pineapple juice, lemon juice, 1/2 Grenadine.

FLIP Sloe Gin, milk, 1/2 simple syrup.

FREDRICO Jack Daniel's, Bacardi Rum, orange juice, pineapple juice, passion fruit juice, 2 guava juice.

FRISCO SOUR Bourbon, 1/2 Benedictine, lemon juice, simple syrup, fill with club soda.

FROZEN RYE Seagram's VO, orange juice, splash Grenadine.

GIBSON 2 Gin, (Dry Vermouth optional), onions.

GIMLET Gin, 1/2 Rose's Lime Juice.

GIN FIZZ Gin, lemon juice, simple syrup, dash milk, fill with club soda. For Fizzes you need a Hamilton-Beach Malt Maker Machine. Blend everything but the club soda and add it last.

GIN & TONIC Gin, fill with Quinine Water (Tonic), squeeze lime.

GIN BUCK Gin, fill with Ginger Ale.

GIN RICKEY Gin, fill with Club Soda.

GIN SONIC Gin, fill with Club Soda and Tonic.

GIN SOUR Gin, lemon juice, simple syrup.

GLENLIVET MIST Glenlivet on shaved ice.

GOLDEN CADILLAC Galliano, 1/2 White Creme de Cacao, milk.

GOLDEN DREAM Galliano, 1/2 Cointreau, 1/2 orange juice, milk.

GOLDEN FIZZ Gin, lemon juice, simple syrup, egg yolk, dash milk, strain in tall glass, fill with Club Soda.

GOLDEN GOPHER Galliano, Drambuie, Scotch.

GRASSHOPPER Green Creme de Menthe, White Creme de Cacao, milk.

GUAVA DAIQUIRI Rum, lemon juice, simple syrup, guava juice.

HANGOVER HELPER Gin, Ginger Ale, 1/2 fresh banana, 3 drops bitters.

HARBOR LIGHTS Galliano, 1/2 Brandy.

HARVEY WALLBANGER Vodka, Galliano, fill with orange juice.

HANNA HO Rum, fill with pineapple juice, float Dark Rum, and squeeze lime.

HEMMINGWAY CUBA LIBRA Juice of whole lime, equal parts Rum and Coke.

HERBIE SPECIAL 1/2 Rum, 1/2 Vodka, 1/2 Apricot Brandy, 1/2 simple syrup, Rose's Lime Juice, dash cinnamon.

HIGHLAND FLING Scotch, Sweet Vermouth, dash Angostura bitters, fill with Club Soda.

HILTY DILTY Apricot Brandy, 1/2 Rose's Lime Juice, dash Grenadine.

HONOLULU COOLER Southern Comfort, 1/2 Rose's Lime Juice, fill with pineapple juice.

HORSE'S NECK 2 Seagram's VO, ginger ale poured on twisted orange rind.

HUNTER COCKTAIL Seagram's VO, 1/2 Cherry Brandy.

IRISH COFFEE Bushmill's Irish Whiskey, 1/2 Kahlua, 1/2 simple syrup, fill with hot coffee, top with whipped cream.

ITALIAN HEATHER COCKTAIL Scotch, 1/2 Galliano.

ITALIAN STINGER Brandy, 1/2 Galliano.

JAMAICAN COFFEE Tia Maria, fill with coffee.

KALYPSO COCKTAIL 1/2 Meyer's Rum, 1/2 Vodka, lemon juice, simple syrup, pineapple juice.

KEIKI POO Rum, lemon juice, coconut syrup, 2 orange juice.

KIAHA Rum, 1/2 Kahlua, milk, coconut syrup.

KING ALPHONSE Dark Creme de Cacao, float milk off back of bar spoon.

KNUCKLEHEAD Scotch, Drambuie.

LEMON COOLER Southern Comfort, fill with Bitter Lemon.

LEMON JUICE What is the one food that doesn't spoil? Lemon juice. So many drinks are made with lemon juice and simple syrup. Something sweet and something sour tricks the tongue. It is the secret to Oriental cooking.

LONG ISLAND ICED TEA 1/2 Gin, 1/2 Vodka, 1/2 Rum, 1/2 Triple Sec, 1/2 Tequila, simple syrup, lemon juice, fill with Coca-Cola.

MADRAS Vodka, orange juice, grapefruit juice, cranberry juice. Pour in order without stirring to make designs.

MAI TAI Light Rum, Orange Curacao, 1/2 Orgeat Syrup, 1/2 Okolehau, pineapple juice, orange juice, lemon juice, passion fruit juice, float Dark Rum.

MANHATTAN Bourbon, 1/2 Sweet Vermouth.

MANHATTAN DRY Bourbon, 1/2 Dry Vermouth.

MANHATTAN PERFECT Bourbon, 1/4 Sweet Vermouth, 1/4 Dry Vermouth.

MARGARITA 1-1/2 Tequila, Triple Sec, 1/2 lemon juice, 1/2 Rose's Lime Juice.

MARTINI 2 Gin (Dry Vermouth optional) olives, or lemon twist.

MILITARY SECRET Brandy, lemon juice, Grenadine, milk.

MILK PUNCH Brandy, 1/2 simple syrup, milk.

MIMOSA Champagne, orange juice. Pour champagne glass half-full of orange juice, fill with Champagne.

MINT JULEP Muddle fresh mint leaves with little simple syrup and water. Strain over crushed ice in tall glass, fill with Old Granddad. Dry a sprig of mint, shake in powdered sugar for garnish.

MOSCONOVITCH Cointreau, 1/2 Brandy.

MUD SLIDE Vodka, Kahlua, Bailey's Irish Cream, scoop vanilla ice cream.

NEGRONI Gin, Campari, Sweet Vermouth.

NEW ORLEANS FIZZ Gin, milk, lemon juice, simple syrup, strain in tall glass, fill with Club Soda add few drops Orange Flower Water.

NEW YORK SOUR Bourbon, lemon juice, simple syrup, orange juice.

OLD FASHION Bourbon, dash simple syrup, dash Angostura Bitters, splash soda.

OMAHA Southern Comfort, Triple Sec, Rose's Lime Juice.

ORANGE BLOSSOM Gin, orange juice, 1/2 simple syrup.

PAHOEHOE Rum, lemon juice, Grenadine, passion fruit juice.

PASSION FRUIT DAIQUIRI Rum, lemon juice, simple syrup, passion fruit juice.

PASSION FRUIT MARGARITA Tequila, Triple Sec, lemon juice, simple syrup, passion fruit juice.

PEPPERMINT PATTY Creme de Cacao Dark, White Creme de Menthe.

PERFECT COCKTAIL Gin, 1/4 Sweet Vermouth, 1/4 Dry Vermouth, dash Angostura Bitters.

PINA COLADA Rum, coconut syrup, milk, crushed pineapple. Canned pineapple soaked in sugar has a better taste than fresh pineapple.

PINEAPPLE DAIQUIRI Rum, lemon juice, simple syrup, fresh or crushed pineapple.

PINK GIN Five drops Angostura Bitters to coat glass, short ice (British You Know), 2 Gin.

PINK LADY Gin, milk, 1/2 Grenadine.

PIRATE'S GOLD Rum, Southern Comfort, lemon juice, simple syrup, fill with orange juice.

PLANTER'S PUNCH Rum, fill with orange juice, dash Grenadine, float Meyer's Rum.

POLYNESIAN DAIQUIRI Rum, Triple Sec, lemon juice, Grenadine, guava juice.

PRAIRIE FIRE Tequila, 3 drops Tabasco.

PUZZLER Southern Comfort, fill with pineapple and grapefruit juice.

RAMOS FIZZ Gin, lemon juice, simple syrup, splash milk, whip with ice, strain, fill with Club Soda add four drops Orange Flower Water for bouquet.

ROB ROY Scotch, 1/2 Sweet Vermouth.

ROB ROY DRY Scotch, 1/2 Dry Vermouth.

ROB ROY PERFECT Scotch, 1/4 Sweet Vermouth, 1/4 Dry Vermouth.

ROOT BEER FLOAT Dark Creme de Cacao, milk, fill with Coca-Cola.

RUM RUNNER Rum, Dark Rum, orange juice, lemon juice, simple syrup, passion fruit juice, Orange Curacao, float Blackberry Brandy.

RUSSIAN MULE Tequila, Kahlua.

RUSTY NAIL Scotch, 1/2 Drambuie.

SALTY DOG Vodka, fill with grapefruit juice, salt rim on glass.

SARATOGA COCKTAIL Gin, Brandy, Sweet Vermouth, dash Orange Bitters.

SARATOGA FIZZ Seagram's VO, lemon juice, simple syrup, egg white.

SARATOGA SOUR Seagram's VO, simple syrup, lemon juice.

SCARLETT O'HARA Southern Comfort, simple syrup, lemon juice, Grenadine.

SCREAMING ORGASM Bailey's Irish Cream, Kahlua, Amaretto.

SCORPION Rum, Brandy, Gin, lemon juice, simple syrup, orange juice, dash Grenadine.

SCOTCH SOUR Scotch Whisky, simple syrup, lemon juice.

SCREWDRIVER Vodka, fill with orange juice.

SEA BREEZE Vodka, fill with cranberry juice, float grapefruit juice.

SEPARATOR Kahlua, pour milk over back of bar spoon so it floats and does not mix.

SEX ON THE BEACH Vodka, Peach Schnapps, fill with cranberry and pineapple juice.

SHAMROCK COCKTAIL Old Bushmill's, 1/2 Dry Vermouth, 1/2 Green Creme de Menthe.

SIDECAR 2 Remy Martin V.S.O.P., Cointreau, lemon juice. Shake and strain in glass rimmed with sugar.

SILVER FIZZ Gin, lemon juice, simple syrup, egg white, dash milk, whip with ice, strain into tall glass fill with Club Soda.

SIMPLE SYRUP Fill a measuring cup with sugar. Slowly stir in hot water until the sugar is dissolved. Makes one cup syrup.

SINGAPORE SLING Gin, Grenadine, simple syrup, lemon juice, 1/2 Cherry Herring, float 1/2 Benedictine.

SLOE GIN FIZZ Sloe Gin (This is not Gin, it is made from berries), lemon juice, Grenadine, fill with Club Soda.

SMITH & KERNS Vodka, 1/2 Kahlua, milk, Club Soda.

SPRITZER Pour White Wine and Club Soda at same time to fill glass.

STRAWBERRY DAIQUIRI Rum, lemon juice, simple syrup, 3-5 frozen strawberries. Strawberries frozen in syrup will make a better drink than fresh strawberries. The color is darker and the sugar brings out the flavor of the fruit.

STINGER Brandy, 1/2 White Creme de Menthe.

SUISSESSE Pernod, 1/2 Anisette, egg white.

SWIZZLE Brandy, Rose's Lime Juice, dash Angostura Bitters, fill with Club Soda.

TEQUILA COCKTAIL Tequila, 1/2 Grenadine, 1/2 Rose's Lime Juice.

TEQUILA SUNRISE Tequila, fill with orange juice, splash Grenadine.

TODDY Jack Daniel's, 1/2 simple syrup.

TROPICAL ITCH Jack Daniel's, Meyer's Rum, 3 passion fruit juice, 3 drops bitters, Orange Curacao, float Bacardi 151 Rum.

VELVET HAMMER Dry Vermouth, 1/2 Creme de Cassis, fill with Club Soda.

VODKA SOUR Vodka, simple syrup, lemon juice.

WARD 8 Seagram's VO, simple syrup, lemon juice, 1/2 grenadine.

WHISKEY SOUR Jack Daniel's, simple syrup, lemon juice.

WHITE LADY Gin, 1/2 Cointreau, milk.

WHITE RUSSIAN Vodka, 1/2 Kahlua, milk.

WHITE SPIDER Vodka, 1/2 White Creme de Menthe, milk.

WHITE WHALE Galliano, milk.

YELLOW MONKEY Vodka, Galliano.

ZOMBIE Rum, Dark Rum, 151 Rum, Falernum, pineapple juice, Rose's Lime Juice.

ONE-LINERS

One-liners are opening gambits. They are bridges in conversation, spanning pregnant moments. One-liners are catalyst; they make things happen.

All great people speak in one-liners. Go back and read their quotes. A bartender needs one-liners because the audience has a short attention span. The longer the joke, the funnier it had better be. It is better to tell a bunch of short jokes, ferret out what the crowd finds funny, and exploit those subjects. You can gauge your popularity by the number of fingers being waved at you. A good indicator is if the crowd turns ugly, you may want to change the subject.

When someone sits down, ask him or her, "Hello. Are you thirsty, or serious?" If a man orders two drinks turn to his wife and ask, "Anything for you?"

Always sell up. If someone orders a beer, pour it for him or her. Then study the glass and ask, "How long has the horse been sick?"

If the restaurant is open ask, "Do you want lunch?" and follow with, "We recommend you eat wherever you go." Subliminal messages work. "It takes a lot of calories to run that personality."

If some dude asks, "Do you serve sandwiches?"

Tell him, "We serve everybody."

When you give someone a bowl of taro chips say, "They are not very good, but they are free." If someone complains about the prices tell him or her, "It costs big money to have me here telling you these lame jokes. Besides, if the price quoted makes you buckle in the knee, then you know you are in West Hawaii. You can go farther but you can't pay more." Most humans will warm to your honesty. Your sincerity will be in doubt.

You should have five one-liners ready at all times and use them in conversation. The fun is steering the conversation through the garden and down the path to where the one-liner is waiting. Be patient. Let the crowd keep up, then surprise them. Here are five to start with:

1. You should always follow your dream. Unless it is the one where you are at work in your underwear, during a fire drill.

2. If you always stop and smell the roses, you will eventually inhale a bee.

3. When someone cuts you off in traffic you should turn the other cheek. Nothing gets the point across like a proper mooning.

4. When I am feeling down, I like to whistle. It makes the neighbor's dog run to the end of his chain and gag.

5. It is always darkest before dawn, and that is the best time to steal your neighbor's newspaper.

Johnny Carson says you must remember everything funny you have ever heard. Someday you will use it. One-liners are funny because they are clever, true, and thought provoking, interesting, shocking or surprising. One-liners depend on the other person's intellect. You can build this intellect by introducing facts and then using the line. To educate the public is futile, but you can set them up for a joke.

Bartenders stand over an ice well. Did you know that Eskimos have 200 words for ice? Do you know why Eskimos wash their clothes in Tide? It is too cold out tide. Do you know how to make ice with holes in it? Use Holy Water. You can be on a roll by knowing three jokes on any subject. These are the lines, from the public domain, to make it roll:

How goes your battle against sobriety?

The rat race is over, the rats won.

My wife makes Rum. I love her still.

You can sell anything once.

Leave them laughing, but get the order first.

As you fall break a leg and knock 'em dead.

There is no ice in Poland. They forgot the recipe.

Did you hear about the Polish hockey team? They all drowned at spring training.

I went to the fights and a hockey game broke out.

Why do Canadians make love doggie style? So they can both watch the hockey game.

There is no egg in eggplant, no ham in hamburger, and neither apple nor pine in pineapple.

English muffins were not invented in England.

French fries were not invented in France.

Sweetmeats are candies. Sweetbreads are meat.

Quicksand works slowly. Boxing rings are square.

Eagles may soar, but weasels don't get sucked into jet engines.

It's hard to soar with eagles when you work with turkeys.

Turkeys are well named.

Turkeys will look up in the rain and drown.

When geese fly in V formation it is always longer on the left. Do you know why? There are more geese on the left.

Why do flamingos stand on one leg? They would fall if they raised that other leg.

Guinea pigs are not from Guinea, and are not pigs.

The early bird gets the worm, but the second mouse gets the cheese.

It's a toss up whether the early bird enjoys the worm as much as the late bird enjoys the shut-eye.

When a house burns up, it burns down.

You fill in a form by filling it out.

An alarm clock goes off by going on.

When the stars are out, they are visible. When the lights are out, they are invisible.

What is the speed of dark?

What would the speed of lightning be if it didn't zigzag?

Jupiter weighs over twice as much as all the other known planets combined.

The sun doesn't go down. The earth goes up.

Everything is God's work and the sunset is his signature.

It's a small world. You have to use your elbows a lot.

It's a small world, but I wouldn't want to paint it.

It's a third world after all.

Earth first, we'll mine the other planets later.

Earth is the insane asylum for the universe.

Love is like a roller coaster. When it's good you don't want to get off. When it isn't you can't wait to throw up.

The name Wendy was made up for the book Peter Pan.

Shirley Temple received 135,000 gifts on her eighth birthday.

If you get behind on your Thank You cards you can sit backwards on the toilet and write them out on the tank.

A Rabbi sent to Alaska is called the frozen chosen.

Atheism is a non-prophet organization. I was going to join, but they don't have holidays.

Coca-Cola was originally green. Iceland consumes more per capita than any other nation.

Dr. Pepper is the oldest soft drink.

Ginger Ale has the most potassium.

Every day more money is printed for Monopoly than the US Treasury.

It is possible to lead a cow upstairs but not downstairs.

Firehouses had circular stairways because the horses learned to walk up the staircases.

The Hawaiian alphabet has 12 letters.

The dot over the letter "i" is called a tittle.

The groove under your nose is called the Phillip's groove.

Men can read smaller print than women; women can hear better.

Intelligent people have more zinc and copper in their hair.

There is nobody dumber than an educated man, once you get him off the subject he is educated on.

The first novel written on a typewriter was Tom Sawyer.

A duck's quack doesn't echo.

I am like the farmer's duck. I don't give a quack.

The San Francisco cable cars are the only mobile National Monuments.

Did you hear about San Francisco? They had a drive-by slapping.

Do you know the nice thing about homosexual love? Afterwards you can have an intelligent conversation.

The airplane Buddy Holly died in was named American Pie.

An ostrich's eye is bigger than its brain.

The longest recorded flight of a chicken is 13 seconds.

I saw a chicken the other day that only had feathers on one side. The outside.

How many doors are on a chicken coop? Two, if there were four it would be a chicken sedan.

What's a Henway? About three pounds.

Birds of a feather flock together. The assholes of this world find each other enchanting.

Never get into a pissing contest with skunks.

All snakes can swim.

Some snakes you step over.

If a male goat is called a ram, and a female donkey is called an ass, why is a ram in the ass called a goose?

Get down goose bumps.

I hate goose bumps on sunburn.

You can use the inside of a banana peel on sunburn.

More people are killed annually in accidents with donkeys than in plane crashes.

They are trying to pass a helmet law for horses.

I came. I saw. I split.

There is a time to love, a time to hate, a time to split and this is it.

Sometimes you have to lose to win.

To always win you must never lose.

It takes a smart man to know when to bail.

Everything in life is timing.

One out of every five miles of interstate highway must be straight enough to land planes.

The name Jeep comes from the army's abbreviation for "General Purpose" vehicle, G.P.

Join the Army, meet interesting people, and kill them.

Who is General Failure and why is he reading my hard disc?

The pentagon has twice as many bathrooms as necessary. It was built for segregation.

Why is there a Navy? To give the Marine Corps someone to dance with.

Why does a Marine have one more brain cell than a horse? So he won't shit during the parade.

Why does a sailor leave a pair of boots at the foot of his wife's bed? He knows a Marine would rather shine shoes than make love.

Take a sailor to dinner and keep him for breakfast.

Happy sailors dancing on a sinking ship.

The Marines are the last to know and the first to go.

The Marines are the first to fight, even if they have to start it themselves.

The Queen Elizabeth II gets six inches per gallon of diesel.

Cat's urine glows under a blacklight.

I like cats. Let's exchange recipes.

Cats...the other white meat.

Ask me about microwaving cats for fun and profit.

Why did God invent people? Something for cats to ignore.

Any time your cat looks at you it is sizing you up for an attack.

Cats go to the lap of the sickest person in the room.

I feel like a fugitive from the law of averages.

I am so dull I bore myself.

The best way to win an argument is to be right.

I can read your mind, when there is something on it.

The more you change your mind the cleaner it will be.

The mind loves routine.

I used to have an open mind, but my brains kept falling out.

Of all the things I've lost, I miss my mind the most.

When I'm not in my right mind, my left mind gets pretty crowded.

If the right side of the brain controls the left side of the body, then only left-handed people are in their right mind.

Polar bears are left-handed.

Where does a polar bear keep his money? In a snow bank.

My mind not only wanders, sometimes it leaves completely.

Sometimes I wonder. The rest of the time I don't know.

If I had your mind, I would want to be out of it too.

What is whack? When you are out of whack, what are you out of?

Why do psychics have to ask you for your name? Why do they have to advertise?

I almost had a psychic girlfriend, but we broke it off before we met.

All those who believe in ESP raise your hand. All those who believe in psychokinetics raise my hand.

Help wanted, Telepathy: You know where to apply.

I don't suffer from insanity; I enjoy every minute of it.

I am not a complete idiot. Some parts are missing.

Allow me to introduce my selves.

The paranoid schizophrenic says, "Go away and stop leaving me alone."

You are jealous because the voices only talk to me.

I can't come to work today. The voices told me to stay home and clean the weapons.

I have matches to burn.

Smoking is a dying art.

Soon you will only be able to smoke out behind the barn where it all started.

As long as you can think, you ought to drink.

You can only drink as long as you can remember your room number.

We call our menu, person-you. We are politically correct. Notice the person-hole covers.

I went to a wine tasting the other night. I cut my lip on a paper sack.

When it comes to wine, put a cork in it.

This wine is arrogant yet reptilian.

The aphrodisiac dose of wine is two ounces.

You get a man full of food and wine, what's the next thing on his mind?

At the winery the employees must wash their feet before returning to work.

At the winery the rumor is, "Don't trust anyone whose name ends in a vowel."

Beer, it's not just for breakfast anymore.

Beer is the reason I get up every afternoon.

Beer has been helping ugly people have sex since 1843.

Beauty is in the eye of the beer holder.

What does it say on the bottom of a Polish beer bottle? Open other end.

I killed a six-pack just to watch it die.

Bad luck is when your joint falls in your beer, on the way to work, and you ruin them both.

If it weren't for bad luck I wouldn't have any.

It could be worse. It could be raining.

Every silver lining has a cloud.

I feel more like I do now than I did.

It will feel better when it quits hurting.

Jesus is coming! Everybody look busy.

Look busy every chance you get.

We are born free and taxed to death.

Never stand if you can sit. Never sit if you can lie down. Never lie down awake if you can sleep.

Sleep is overrated. You get all you need after death.

Sleep is a short form of death.

Snooze you lose.

I sleep like a baby. I wake up crying every hour.

If a light sleeper sleeps better with a light on, does a hard sleeper sleep better with a window open?

Some people are alive only because it's illegal to kill them.

A dolt is someone with the mentality between that of a horse and a carrot.

He couldn't pour piss out of a boot with directions on the heel.

Don't take life too seriously. You won't get out alive.

I want a meaningful overnight relationship.

I need a woman really bad. Are you really bad?

I used to have a handle on life, but it broke.

Isn't it funny how when you are holding all the cards in life, everyone else is playing chess?

Hang up and drive.

Pardon my driving. I am reloading.

Cover me while I change lanes.

If your brakes don't work, you have to have a horn.

The horn is broken. Watch for finger.

The more you complain the longer God lets you live.

Smoke 'em if you got 'em.

If you smoke after sex, you are doing it too fast.

Men use love to get sex. Women use sex to get love.

The doctor asked are you having safe sex? I'm using a condom and a glove. What about your partner? Partner?

Love is a long and slender thing.

Don't drink and drive. You might hit a bump and spill your drink.

We are born naked, wet, and hungry. Then things get worse.

Always remember you are unique, just like everyone else.

A lottery is a tax on people who are bad at math.

There is always death and taxes. However, death doesn't get worse every year.

Disneyland is a people trap run by a mouse.

What is the hardest thing about milking a mouse? Getting the bucket under it.

Friends help you move. Real friends help you move bodies.

Friends may come and go, but enemies accumulate.

You never know who your friends are.

Good girls let you. Bad girls help you.

Good girls go to heaven. Bad girls go everywhere.

You know you are getting old when you see a girl you used to know and it's her daughter.

Consciousness is that annoying time between naps.

A clear conscience is usually the sign of a bad memory.

A conscience is what hurts when all your other parts feel so good.

Ever stop to think, and forget to start again?

I like you, but I wouldn't want to see you working with subatomic particles.

Sex on television can't hurt you unless you fall off.

Work hard. Millions on welfare are depending on you.

I work like I am paid: a little every two weeks.

Raising teenagers is like nailing Jell-O to a tree.

Laughing helps. It's like jogging on the inside.

If you are still smiling, you haven't heard all the facts.

When everything is coming your way, you're in the wrong lane.

If everything seems to be going well, you have obviously overlooked something.

By the time you make ends meet, they move the ends.

The light at the end of the tunnel is a freight train coming your way.

It is dryer than a popcorn fart.

It is dryer than a cornflake on a toast sandwich.

Tighter than Dick's hat band.

Tougher than a boot.

Slicker than Vaseline on a doorknob.

Hear about the newlyweds who got Vaseline mixed up with wallpaper paste? All their wallpaper fell off.

Colder than a witch's tit.

The colder the X-ray table, the more of your body is required to be on it.

Harder than a whore's heart.

The hardness of the butter is inversely proportional to the softness of the bread.

Wetter than a well digger's shovel.

I had a Tropical Itch, but Cortisone cleared it up.

The severity of the itch is proportional to the reach.

I am busier than a one-armed paperhanger with the seven-year itch.

What's the one thing a one-armed man can't do? Put his cuff link on.

How do you get a one-armed man out of a tree? Wave to him.

I was lost in thought. It was unfamiliar territory.

A conclusion is the place where you tired of thinking.

Keep thinking. That's what you are good at.

We all have to believe in something even if it's wrong.

I believe you should have another beer.

I have a photographic memory. I am just out of film.

Seen it all, done it all, can't remember most of it.

I take Ginkgo Biloba for my memory. If I can remember to take it.

I feel like I'm diagonally parked in a parallel universe.

For every action, there is an equal and opposite criticism.

No act of kindness will go unpunished.

I feel like I am 17, and there is something wrong.

Sometimes I feel like a 20-year-old, but there is never one available.

When shooting a mime, do you need a silencer?

A mime is a terrible thing to waste.

If a mime is arrested do they tell him he has the right to talk?

Those who live by the sword get shot by those who don't.

He's not dead. He is electroencephalographically challenged.
She's always late. Her ancestors arrived on the June Flower.
You have the right to remain silent. Anything you say will be misquoted and used against you.
I only open my mouth to change feet.
A closed mouth gathers no feet.
He has hoof in mouth disease.
The ocean looks really full today. How much fuller would it be without sponges?
Save the whales. Collect the whole set.
If swimming makes you thin, how do you account for whales?
How do you circumcise a whale? You start with four skin divers.
What do whales do after sex? They swim off and smoke a herring.
What's purple and sits on the bottom of the ocean? Moby Prune.
On the other hand you have different fingers.
At no time do my hands leave my wrists.
The hand is quicker than the ear.
Shake an old cowhand.
Change is inevitable. Except from a vending machine.
Change is growth. If your growth changes, get it checked.
An erection is not considered personal growth.
A day without sunshine is like night.
What caused the Dark Ages? The Y1K bug.
A day without a Fredrico is like a tomorrow without a hangover.
A hangover is the wrath of grapes.
What's purple and goes bang, bang, bang, bang? A four door grape.
What's green and rides a horse? Roy Asparagus.
Where was Roy Rogers going when he put all of his trash on Trigger? To de dump, to de dump to de dump, dump, dump.
I don't drink this stuff. I see what it does to my customers.
I will have whatever the lady on the floor is having.
My drinks make you see double and think single.
Sometimes too much to drink is not enough.
Drink to remember, not to forget.
If you have lime with the drink you won't get heartburn.

You can never give up your fight against scurvy in the tropics.
I am not very good. I don't do much. I am just here to separate you from your dollar.
I am alive and almost well.
Don't pay the ransom. I've escaped.
A statistician is someone without the personality to be an accountant.
Forty-two point seven percent of all statistics are made up on the spot.
Seventy percent of all drownings are due to alcohol in the blood.
An accountant's idea of a seven-course meal is a six-pack and a doughnut.
I don't find it hard to meet expenses. They're everywhere.
How come there is so much of the month left at the end of the money?
If you think nobody cares about you, try missing a couple of payments.
Bills travel through the mail at twice the speed of checks.
How can I be out of money? I still have checks left.
Inflation is when the buck doesn't stop anywhere.
Despite the cost of living, it remains popular.
The only time to save money is when you have some.
Anybody can make money. It takes a frugal man to hold on to it.
For every man teaching his son to be thrifty there is a woman teaching her daughter to be extravagant.
An old man figured out a way to take it all with him. He walked up to the Pearly Gates dragging a trunk. The angel looked in it and asked, "What are you going to do with all that pavement?"
Count your change, no refunds after five minutes.
Money is no problem. Lack of money is a problem.
The reason you have small problems is because you are not thinking big.
If money is the root of all evil, what is the bloom?
What this world needs is a good five-cent nickel.
Borrow money from pessimists, they don't expect it back.
A fool and his money are soon invited out.
Nothing is foolproof to a sufficiently talented fool.

Nothing is impossible for those who don't have to do it.

The next time someone tells you nothing is impossible, ask them to dribble a football.

The trouble with life is you're halfway through it before you realize it's a do-it-yourself project.

Stop wasting time on projects that benefit no one including yourself.

I intend to live forever--so far so good.

If I knew I was going to live this long I would have taken better care of myself.

Life's middle age is when you choose the cereal for the fiber and not the toy.

Life's golden age is when the kids are too old to need baby-sitters and too young to borrow the family car.

Life's metal age is when you have silver in your hair, gold in your teeth and lead in your ass.

Life's a bitch and then you die.

Where there is a will, there is a probate.

He died, but it was nothing serious.

May you be in heaven an hour before the devil knows you're dead.

I want to die peacefully in my sleep like my grandfather. Not like his four screaming passengers.

My favorite headstone reads, "I told you I was sick."

Life's a crapshoot. Shake 'em and roll.

Life is a short span of time between birth and death.

That's life. She is over before she begins.

We are born alone and we die alone.

We all end up in a single bed.

Today's mighty oak is just yesterday's nut that held its ground.

Nothing pays off like persistence.

You can get used to hanging if you hang long enough.

Some people would bitch if they were hung with a new rope.

Complaints must be viewed as an opportunity and not a problem.

Eat a live toad first thing in the morning, and nothing worse can happen to you the rest of the day.

You have to kiss a lot of frogs to find a prince.

Families are like fudge...mostly sweet with a few nuts.

Doing a business deal in San Francisco is like dealing with a granola bar. Once you get past the fruits and nuts you have to put up with the flakes.

He is so far out the air is thin.

Sometimes I am right on sometimes I am more on.

You can go so far back on his family tree you will find the sap.

Work is for people who don't know how to fish.

Have you ever been too drunk to fish?

Hear about the fish that swam into the wall? He said, "Dam."

When fish die they roll over and float to the surface. It's their way of sinking to the bottom.

You don't know what you're missing. It's the best part of the fish.

What's the difference between a guitar and fish? You can't tuna fish.

A goldfish learns everything new every five minutes.

Beavers are the best dam builders.

Hard work is a future payoff. Laziness pays off now.

Ambition is a poor excuse for not having enough sense to be lazy.

Reality is for people who don't do drugs.

Trying to make it real compared to what?

Drugs will get you through times of no money better than money will get you through times of no drugs.

You are making too much money when all you are buying is cocaine.

Cocaine won't make you crazy and weed won't make you lazy.

Most heroin addicts started out on mother's milk.

Drugs may lead to nowhere, but at least it's the scenic route.

Exhibiting a modicum of will power?

You are in charge of how you want to feel.

What is the best thing that ever came out of Texas? Route 66.

Happiness is Lubbock, Texas in the rear-view mirror.

Some places look better looking back.

Texas women walk across your heart like it was Texas.

You could stab me all day and not find a heart.

She took everything but her memory.

If you must choose between two evils, pick the one you've never tried before.

I can't wait for the melting pot. Let's boil them in oil.

Support bacteria--they're the only culture some people have.

There is an air of culture about this place...agriculture.

Prevent inbreeding: Ban country music.

Coming in on a wing and a prayer.

Before you do anything, pray.

As long as there are tests, there will be prayer in public schools.

There is nothing wrong with school. It is just the principal of the thing.

I remember the fifth grade. It was the best three years of my life.

If all the girls in my graduating class were laid end to end I wouldn't doubt it.

There were 26 kids in my graduating class. I have always been proud to say I was in the top 25.

Happiness is a belt-fed weapon.

I would kill for a Nobel Peace Prize.

Guns don't kill people, postal workers do.

Everyone should own a gun. They should ban bullets.

I got a gun for my wife. Best trade I ever made.

I didn't fight my way to the top of the food chain to be a vegetarian.

Can vegetarians eat animal crackers?

When the chips are down the buffalo is empty.

If we aren't supposed to eat animals, why are they made of meat?

Is shell-less turtle homeless or just naked?

Where do you find a turtle with no legs? Exactly where you left it.

What do you call a cow with no legs? Ground beef.

What do you call a cow with two legs? Lean beef.

The cows go by but the bull never stops.

The older the bull the harder the horn.

What do you call a deer with no eyes? No eye deer.

What do you call a deer with no eyes standing still? Still no eye deer.

What do you call a dog with no legs? It doesn't matter he can't come anyway.

What do you do with a dog with no legs? You take him out for a drag.

I spilled some spot remover on my dog, and now he's gone.
Youth is wasted on the young.
There is too much youth. How about a fountain of smart?
Rainy days and automatic weapons always get me down.
Do you think the rain will hurt the rhubarb? Not if it's in cans.
Time is the best teacher. Unfortunately it kills all its students.
Experience is a bad teacher. It gives you the test first, then the lesson.
Experience is something you don't get until just after you need it.
It's too bad opportunity doesn't come with directions.
Opportunity makes the thief.
A lock just keeps an honest man honest.
Everybody wants something for nothing.
Rich people, poor people, sooner or later everybody bums cigarettes.
The three great equalizers in life are pain, suffering, and death.
The three rings of marriage are the engagement ring, the wedding ring, and the suffering.
In just two days, tomorrow will be yesterday.
Time is going to go by whether we wait or not.
Time flies whether you're having fun or not.
Time wounds all heels.
Every day will have its dog.
This day is a total waste of makeup.
This experience is a waste of Elavil.
Make yourself at home. Clean my kitchen.
Home is where the hang-ups are.
A man's home is his hassle.
Who are these kids and why are they calling me Mom?
This isn't work. It's Hell with fluorescent lighting.
A cubicle is just a padded cell without a door.
Therapy is expensive; popping bubble wrap is cheap. You choose.
I started out with nothing and have most of it left.
I pretend to work. They pretend to pay me.
Do you know why they only give us a half-hour for lunch? So they don't have to retrain us.

Sarcasm is just one more service we offer.

The obnoxious shall be treated with obnoxion.

So much for being witty and engaging.

Whatever kind of look you were going for, you missed.

Suburbia is where they tear out the trees and then name the streets after them.

Contractors have a recessive gene that makes it so they can lie to people, not show up and run rust by you.

I am just working here until a good fast-food job opens up.

Can I trade this job for what's behind door number two?

It was the squeaky wheel that got the grease. Now the head that sticks up gets nailed down.

I am so far down I have to look up to see the bottom.

Next time I am picking rich parents.

I'm not your type. I'm not inflatable.

You have the qualities I admire in a woman. Sex organs.

Wink, I'll do the rest.

I am trying to imagine you with a personality.

Nice perfume. Must you marinate in it?

So you're a feminist. Isn't that cute?

You look like shit. Is that the style now?

It's hard to get happy after that one.

What am I, an information booth?

Not everybody can wear those colors.

Fashion says, "Me too." Style says, "Only me."

Don't worry. I forgot your name, too.

I'm sick of the way people keep having sex without me.

To all you virgins out there, thanks for nothing.

Virginity causes cancer. Join your cancer crusade.

Too many freaks, not enough circuses.

Chaos, panic and disorder. My work goes on.

I am the most responsible guy here. Even if I am not here I am responsible.

Ambivalent? Well, yes and no. Give me ambiguity or give me something else.

Everyone thinks I'm psychotic, except for my friends deep inside the earth.

Is it time for your medication or mine?

We take drugs seriously at my house.

Is the going up worth the coming down?

Does this condom make me look fat?

Work is the curse of the drinking class.

Don't curse, it sounds like hell and doesn't do a damn bit of good.

I thought I wanted a career. Turns out I just wanted paychecks.

Many people quit looking for work when they find a job.

I love this job. It's the work I hate.

I'm lucky. I have fun at work.

Wishing without work is like fishing without bait.

You do good work. Bring your lunch tomorrow and I will put you on steady.

It's not me; it's these assholes I work with.

The more you put into anything the more you get out of it.

It's not the hours put into the work, it is the work put into the hours.

We often find our destiny on the road we take to avoid it.

I am getting in shape for summer and Buddha is the shape I've picked.

A balanced diet is a cookie in each hand.

Eat well, stay fit, and die anyway.

I am not tense, just terribly, terribly alert.

I don't have attitude. I have vertigo. It's all pilot talk.

Pilots are just plane people.

I pile it here and I pile it there.

There is too much blood in my alcohol system.

I only drink when I am alone or with someone.

I asked him, "How much do you drink a day, about a pint?"

He said, "Hell, sonny, I spill more than that."

Pigs don't have sweat glands.

Horses are bad news at both ends.

Horses, when it rains you smell them.

A man alone is in bad company.

You can tell one who boozes, by the company she chooses.

Maybe we will and maybe we won't.

You go to your church, and I'll go to mine.

Here is to honor. Get on her and stay on her.

She was a housekeeper. Every time she got a divorce she kept the house.

Don't give your wife enough money to hire a lawyer.

Do you know why married men die younger than single men? They want to.

They threw me out of that mental hospital. I was depressing the other patients.

Depression is merely anger without enthusiasm.

If someone with multiple personalities threatens suicide, is it considered a hostage situation?

She walked in and said, "The good news is the air-bag worked."

My country right or wrong, my mother drunk or sober.

My mother is 85 years old and never needed glasses. She drinks straight out of the bottle.

The first girl I was ever intimate with, really had sex with, was a real screamer. You would think she had never seen a knife before.

It's the dull knife that cuts you.

Never take a laxative and a sleeping pill on the same night.

Never rent two sailors and a chicken on the same night.

Never squat with spurs on.

Never fry bacon naked.

Never pet a burning dog.

Let sleeping dogs lie.

Be nice to your family. Next to your dog they are the first ones to forgive your transgressions.

Don't trust anybody named Lucky or Ace.

What's the difference between Ass and Ace? Just the way it's spelled Ace.

Don't play cards with anyone named after a city.

Don't do card tricks for the guys you play poker with.

A Smith & Wesson beats four of a kind.

Liquor in the front, poker in the rear.

You spit on the floor and you are out the door.

Things come out of you the way they go in you. Beware of large bananas.

What's yellow and goes "click, click?" A ballpoint banana.

You should always take bananas into the jungle so the monkeys will be on your side.

You can only tell 50% about a woman from the back.

Keep your eye on the doughnut and not the hole.

What happens to the doughnut hole after you eat the doughnut?

Keep drinking; I am a still making sense.

Let me know if I am going too fast for you.

Know any fast girls? Know any slow ones?

How do you tell when you're out of invisible ink?

A shin is a device for finding furniture in the dark.

If Barbie is so popular, why do you have to buy her friends?

Did you hear about divorce Barbie? It comes with all of Ken's things.

Do you know why divorces cost so much? They're worth it.

Dancing is a perpendicular expression of a horizontal desire.

Boycott shampoo! Demand the real poo.

What happens if you get scared half to death twice?

If at first you don't succeed, try not to look astonished.

If at first you don't succeed, destroy all evidence that you tried.

If at first you don't succeed, then skydiving definitely isn't for you.

Why don't blind people take up skydiving? It scares the hell out of their dog.

Did you hear about the skydiver whose parachute didn't open? He jumped to a conclusion.

You can't argue with success.

My karma ran over my dogma.

You never really learn to swear until you learn to drive.

I drive way too fast to worry about cholesterol.

When in doubt gas it.

Faster you fool.

The fastest I ever went I fell off.

Nobody ever looks happy on a bicycle.

They will never take me alive.

You call this living?

Hold my beer and watch this.

The right of way is always given, never taken.

Never trust a signal. It may have been left on from a previous turn.

She drives like old people screw. Not very well and not very often.

If you don't recognize road rage then you probably cause it.

I put up a good fight for the first 20 feet.

I had to bang my face against his knee to appease him.

I was doing all right until somebody stepped on my tongue.

How much do you know about street fighting?

When the cops came we got carried away.

The problem with the gene pool is there is no lifeguard.

How do you tell the difference between male chromosomes and female chromosomes? You pull down their genes.

Half the people you know are below average.

You spend one-seventh of your life on Monday.

I plan to be spontaneous tomorrow.

The sooner you fall behind, the more time you'll have to catch up.

A papa tomato, a momma tomato and a baby tomato are walking. The mother goes back and stomps on the baby and says, "Ketchup."

Ninety-nine percent of the lawyers give the rest a bad name.

Engage your brain before operating your mouth.

Every time you speak, your mind is on parade. It never ceases to amaze me what parades through your mind.

Keep talking. I am listening.

Some people talk all the time and don't say anything.

Some people say little and mean a lot.

Your ears never stop growing.

Make sure the bridge is there before you cross it.

Being positive is being wrong at the top of your voice.

Life is like a movie. It is whatever you can cop to on the set.

There are no leading men in life, only actors.

If all the world is a stage, where does the audience sit?

You should be on the stage. There is one leaving at noon.

Go right through that door and keep going.

Take a walk until your hat floats.

You always find lost things the last place you look.

You can't get lost. There is only one road. You are either on it or looking for it.

You don't know what you've got until it's gone.

It is the search for things that makes life interesting.

You get more exercise when you are forgetful.

The best things in life aren't things.

When others go wrong you don't have to go along.

Humor is the last refuge of sanity.

He who laughs last thinks slowest.

He who hesitates is probably right.

He who hesitates is lost in city traffic.

He who loses his temper loses all.

I get so mad I could crush a butterfly.

Don't get mad; get even.

Some people hang onto life and sanity with the thinnest of threads.

As you travel through life you can either make dust or eat dust.

Make like a horse turd and hit the trail.

There is no evidence to support the notion that life is serious.

It is easier to get forgiveness than permission.

Always yield to temptation. It may not pass your way again.

Opportunities always look bigger going than coming.

Junk is something you throw away two weeks before you need it.

There is always one more imbecile than you counted on.

Artificial intelligence is no match for natural stupidity.

Always try to be modest and proud of it.

Two wrongs are only the beginning.

If it's not broke, you're not trying.

No one is listening until you make a mistake.

It's better to be heard and remembered rather than seen and forgotten.

People tend to forget about you until you do something unforgettable.

Success occurs in private and failure in full view.

The only substitute for good manners is fast reflexes.
Indecision is the key to flexibility.
It is nice to have a goal.
I didn't plan to fail. I failed to plan.
You can't tell which way the train went by looking at the track.
If east is east and west is west and never the twain shall meet, why do we have so many twain wrecks?
Even if you are on the right track you will get run over if you just stand there.
There is no substitute for a genuine lack of preparation.
Happiness is the remission of pain.
Pain hurts.
It hurts to be on the cutting edge.
If you are not living on the edge you are taking up too much room.
I am worried I won't always be this happy.
Worry is what the mind does when it can't make up its mind.
Don't worry be happy.
These are the good old days.
Nostalgia isn't what it used to be.
First you get the facts, it doesn't matter what you do with them.
The facts, although interesting, are irrelevant.
Don't cloud my mind with facts.
Anything worth fighting for is worth fighting dirty for.
Anything worth doing is worth overdoing.
Anything can happen and usually does.
There is never time to do it right, but always time to do it over.
Measure twice and cut once.
We cut it off twice and it is still too short.
When all else fails, read the directions.
A human given a chance will assemble it backwards.
Everything should be made as simple as possible, but no simpler.
Keep it simple stupid.
There is no use getting practical now, it is too late.
I have seen the truth and it makes no sense.
Sometimes people tell you the truth and you don't realize it until later.

If you think there is good in everybody, you haven't met everybody.

If you can smile when things go wrong, you have someone in mind to blame.

If you are not playing palace politics you are losing. That's what the winners are doing.

Do unto others before them mothers can do it unto you.

The way to the top is paved with small heads, to step on.

I would like to thank the little people...

Smile, it makes people wonder what you have been up to.

Smile, it's the second best thing you can do with your lips.

The careful application of terror is also a form of communication.

Deny no rumors.

Old truckers never die. They just get a new Peterbilt.

What's the difference between a trucker and a puppy? After six weeks a puppy stops whining.

Chivalry isn't dead it just smells that way.

Smells can trigger memories but memories can't trigger smells.

Never be afraid to try something new. Remember: Amateurs built the ark. Experts built the Titanic.

What kinds of lights were on Noah's ark? Flood lights.

Why didn't they play cards on Noah's ark? There was an elephant on the deck.

An ex is something in the past, and a spurt is a drip under pressure. The pressure builds.

You're all I've got so the pressure is on.

I always wanted to be a procrastinator, never got around to it.

Politicians and diapers have one thing in common. They should both be changed regularly and for the same reason.

How do you tell when a politician is lying? His lips are moving.

We have the best politicians money can buy.

There is nothing you can do about politics, so screw it.

I was a kleptomaniac. Now I take something for it.

If marriage were outlawed, only outlaws would have in-laws.

Blessed are those who hunger and thirst, for they are sticking to their diets.

Life is an endless struggle full of frustrations and challenges, but eventually you find a hair stylist you like.

She spends so much time in the beauty shop we call her, "Bleaches and cream."

Time may be a great healer, but it is a lousy beautician.

It's frustrating when you know all the answers, but nobody bothers to ask you the questions.

The more you know, the more you realize there is to know.

A smart man knows everything. A wise man knows everybody.

Some people grow up as they grow old. Some people just grow old.

You know you are getting old when someone says; "Nice alligator shoes" and you're barefoot.

You know you are getting old when you bend over to tie your shoes and look around to see if there is anything else you can do while you are down there.

What's the difference between old people and young people? Young people don't moan when they have to move.

How do you make a hormone? Don't pay her.

Why did they invent whiskey? So old people wouldn't have to live in pain.

You don't stop laughing because you grow old. You grow old because you stop laughing.

Time spent laughing is time spent with the Gods.

An optimist thinks that this is the best possible world. A pessimist fears that this is true.

You cannot make someone love you. All you can do is stalk them and hope they give in.

No matter how much you care some people are just idiots.

It takes years to build up a trust, but only suspicion to destroy it.

You can get by on charm for 15 minutes, after that you better have a great body.

We are responsible for what we do, unless we are celebrities.

You are responsible for your offspring until you or they die.

The people you care most about in life will be taken from you too soon. The less important ones just never go away.

Don't trust people, they have a way of dying on you.

We all march to the tune of a different bummer.
No one has a monopoly on misery. I had to pull on a wet pair of Levi's once.
The end of the world comes for each of us one at a time.
There is only one woman who always knows where her husband is...the widow.
Aim to be the person your dog thinks you are.
Learn a lesson from your dog. Take a long walk everyday.
My grandfather was an old Indian fighter. My grandmother was an old Indian.
My grandmother started walking when she was 80. Now we have no idea where she is.
Get out of the oven granny; you are too old to ride the range.
Accept that some days you are the pigeon, and some days you are the statue.
I can only please one person per day. Today is not your day.
Tomorrow isn't looking good either.
Look in this eye and count the people who care.
On the keyboard of life, always keep one finger on the escape key.
Someday you will look back on this and plow into a parked car.
I will cherish this hour for minutes.
There are few personal problems that cannot be solved through a suitable application of high explosives.
I want enough TNT to put this Volkswagen in orbit.
Modern computers make it easier to get into trouble than Tequila and handguns.
Good news is life's way of keeping you off balance.
If you want to make the Gods laugh, make plans.
I miss my ex-wife but my aim is getting better.
Men continue to have sex with their ex-wives. They like dealing with an established firm.
Stupidity got us into this mess. Why can't it get us out?
If some women ever had a conversation about what they understood, the silence would be deafening.
She has two brain cells that have yet to meet.
If she ever had an original idea it would die of loneliness.
Loneliness is all it's cracked up to be.

I get about as lonely as the first spider in a new house.

My kid has her mother's brains. I still have mine.

I don't mind going nowhere as long as it's an interesting path.

It's hard to make a comeback when you haven't been anywhere.

This is a dead end job. Where do you go from here?

My inferiority complex is not as good as yours.

I am having an out of money experience.

All things being equal, fat people use more soap.

Marriage is defined as an expensive way to get the laundry done.

A woman marries a man thinking she can change him and she can't.

A man marries a woman hoping she won't change and she does.

I married Miss Right. I didn't know her first name was Always.

My wife tells me when she wants my opinion she will give it to me.

I am somebody at my house. Every night my wife yells, "Will somebody take out the garbage!"

I went home the other night and there was no hot water. I raised hell with the women I live with. I can't do the dishes in cold water. She was out reading the paper. I told her, "I can write my name in the dust on the mantle."

Without looking up she said, "That's why I married a college graduate."

If it weren't for marriage men would go through life thinking they had no faults.

I never knew what real happiness was until I got married. Then it was too late.

An Irish man says, "My wife is an angel."

His friend says, "You're lucky. Mine's still alive."

My wife and I are inseparable. Last week it took four state troopers and a dog.

When we go out I hold her hand. If I let go she starts shopping.

Women love to shop because all the goods are laid out on shelves, or hanging on racks, competing for their attention. They like things to compete for their attention.

Wisdom is knowing where to shop.

Bigamy is having one wife too many. Some say monogamy means the same thing.

The punishment for bigamy is two mothers-in-law.

The most effective way to remember your wife's birthday is to forget it once.

Birthdays are good for you. Statistics show the more you have the longer you live.

If man evolved from apes, why do we still have apes?

Should crematoriums give discounts to burn victims?

Why do they use sterile needles for lethal injections?

Why is there Braille on drive-thru bank machines?

Why did kamikaze pilots wear helmets?

What was the best thing before sliced bread? Seats on plows or pockets on pants?

My favorite cave man is the one who extended mating season to all year.

What did we blame things on before we had computers? Damn Hippies.

Why do they lock gas station rest rooms? Are they afraid someone will clean them?

Would a wing-less fly be called a walk?

What would you do if you see an endangered animal eating an endangered plant?

If a parsley farmer is sued, do they garnish his wages?

Where do forest rangers go to get away from it all?

If a mute swears, does his mother wash his hands with soap?

Isn't it scary that doctors call what they do "practice?"

Four out of five people have trouble with fractions.

If quitters never win, and winners never quit, how do you quit while you are ahead?

What hair color do they list on driver's licenses for bald men?

Men who are bald in front are sexy. Men who are bald in back are thinkers. Men who are bald all over think they're sexy.

He must be a big wheel. His head looks like a hubcap.

Women should put pictures of missing husbands on beer cans.

The best thing a married man can see is when he opens the refrigerator door is his wife's picture on the milk carton.

They should put pictures of criminals on postage stamps so the postmen can look for them while they deliver the mail.

The mail takes so long because the postman has to walk.

Don't accept registered mail; it's never good news.

Never agree to plastic surgery if the doctor's office is full of paintings by Picasso.

Did you hear about the two gay plastic surgeons? They hung each other.

If we are here to help others, what are they here for?

Clones are people too.

Stressed spelled backwards is desserts.

Stress is when you wake up screaming and realize you haven't fallen asleep yet.

No one ever says, "It's only a game" when their team is winning.

If you can't be kind, at least have the decency to be vague.

If you can't convince them with logic, befuddle them with bullshit.

If ignorance is bliss, why aren't more people happy?

Sometimes I wake up grumpy. Other times I let her sleep.

Be nice to your kids. They will pick out your nursing home.

I haven't spoken to my wife in months. She gets mad if I interrupt her.

She can have PMS. I want ESPN.

Never argue with a woman whose voice is lower than yours.

Old people read the Bible like they are booking for finals.

Put decals on slightly crooked and they will come out straight.

Green is ground on Honda.

Cute as a button.

Button, button the folks are coming.

I have a button here. Would you sew a shirt on it?

Don't worry about what people think of you. You will find people are too busy thinking about themselves to think of you.

I got out of medicine; those people are sick.

Medicine is 90% bullshit and 10% drugs. Cut the bullshit and give me the drugs.

Doctors bury their mistakes.

Internists know everything and do nothing.

Surgeons know nothing and do everything.

Pathologists know everything and do everything, just too late.

Do you know the difference between a bartender and a proctologist? A proctologist just has to put up with one asshole at time.

Someone is playing the rectaphone.

If I hadn't had my mouth open I would have got it right in the face.

I told my dentist I didn't have a chance to floss. She said, "That's okay, I didn't have time to wash my hands."

The three rules of oral hygiene. 1. Brush often. 2. Floss regular. 3. Always be polite. There is no use having nice teeth if someone is going to bust them out for you.

Did you hear about the dentist who named his estate Tooth Acres?

You can't outrun a toothache.

What is the hardest thing about doing a root canal on an elephant? Getting it to spit in the little cup.

A lady goes to the dentist and says, "I don't know whether to have a root canal or a baby."

The dentist says, "Let me know. I have to adjust the chair."

A gynecologist is a spreader of old wives tails.

Do you know the difference between a genealogist and a gynecologist? A genealogist looks up the family tree. A gynecologist looks up the family bush.

Did you hear about the gynecologist who had to get a divorce? He was looking up an old girlfriend.

Here's looking up your old address.

What does D.A.M. stand for? Mothers against dyslexia.

Dyslexics of the world, untie.

Did you hear about the dyslexic cop? He was giving tickets for IUDs.

I am not cheap, but I am on special this week.

For the next 15 minutes all drinks regular price.

This bar is so tight we have a happy minute.

What has six legs and a cherry? Three cocktail waitresses and a Tom Collins.

What has two breasts, 16 legs and runs through the forest singing? Snow White and the seven dwarves.

I love defenseless animals, especially in good gravy.

When the gravy turns out thin they call it sauce.

Do you know the difference between a chef and a cook? Tattoos.

The nurse says, "The invisible man is in the waiting room."

The doctor says, "Tell him I can't see him now."

Nurse: "Doctor the patient you just treated fell dead on the sidewalk. What shall we do?"

Doctor: "The first thing you do is turn him around so it looks like he is headed into the office."

Mothers make the best nurses.

How do you tell the head nurse? Dirty knees.

I told the nurse my knee hurt. She asked, "Your right knee, your left knee or your wee knee?"

I had my wife on her knees. She was begging me to come out from under the bed so she could hit me some more.

Don't let the wolf in the door because you are mad at your old lady.

I lost my head.

Here I'll get it.

I lost my train of thought. It must have been a light load.

Does your train of thought have a caboose?

How do you top a train? Tep on de brake.

If everyone in the world would hold hands, close their eyes and visualize world peace, imagine how serene it would be until the looting started.

If a person who studies the weather is called a meteorologist, is a person who studies meteors called a cosmetologist?

How much are the bricks? The more you buy the cheaper they get. Throw them on the truck until they're free.

It's raining like a cow peeing on a flat rock.

A pluvial is a tropical rainstorm.

Vacations are when you check out the rain in other parts of the world.

Beauty is only skin deep but ugly runs clear to the bone.

Uglier than a mud fence.

Uglier than a windrow of assholes.

If my dog's face was that ugly I would shave its ass and make it walk backwards.

Housework makes you ugly.

Heartaches give you gray hair.

Surf Naked.

Not normal is my motto.

Waste not, care less.

What goes around gets dizzy and falls over.

Hard to say.

Sweets for the sweets. Won't you have some of these nuts?

Candy is dandy but liquor is quicker.

Cleanliness is next to impossible around here.

A clean ship is a happy ship.

An empty ship is the devil's playground.

Ship ahoy corduroy.

Where's your anchor clanker?

Why were the Indians the first Americans? They had reservations.

What do you call a white man surrounded by 10 Indians? A bartender.

What is white and sleeps three? The reservation pickup.

Did you hear about the Indian who drank too much tea? He drowned in his teepee.

Did you hear about the Indian who ran into the psychiatrist office screaming, "I am a wigwam I am a teepee?" The doctor said, "Slow down you are two tents."

How many psychiatrists does it take to change a light bulb? Only one but the light bulb really has to want to change.

A man walks into a psychiatrist's office draped in Saran Wrap. The doctor looks up and says, "I can see your nuts."

Why did Cleopatra never see a shrink? She was in de Nile.

My how you talk, and you are somebody's mother.

Women have dreams too.

A farmer is outstanding in his field.

Why do firemen have bigger balls than policemen? They sell more tickets.

Nuke the dolphins.

Blame your parents for what you are. Blame yourself for staying that way.

If we are what we eat, then I am fast, cheap and easy.

You are what you eat off of.

Once on the lips, forever on the hips.

Desserts will show up in the end.

You may not be much, but you're all you've got.

You must take care of yourself if you are going to live forever.

You cannot forget the inner man.

A man needs a maid.

Sex must be play. If it were work, my wife would have the maid do it.

A man without a wife is like a fish without a motorcycle.

How do you make a Harley-Davidson motorcycle go 100 miles-per-hour in a quarter of a mile? You drop it for a quarter of a mile.

What is the difference between a Harley and a Hoover? The dirt bag is on the inside on a Hoover.

Why is a Harley like a hound dog? They both like to ride in trucks. They both leave puddles and they have the same initials.

Loud pipes save lives. They can't see you if they can't hear you.

The volcano is a hole in God's muffler.

The initials HD stand for "Hundred Dollars" at the Harley dealers.

English motorcycles don't leak. They just mark their spot.

Do you know why the English drink warm beer? Their refrigerators are made by Lucas.

Lucas, the prince of darkness.

I had a Jaguar. Inside was a plaque that read, "This darkness provided by Lucas."

Lucas electric devices leak smoke. If you keep the smoke in they work fine.

Do you know why Siamese twins like to visit England? So the other one can drive.

Is everything groovy? This has been a groovy check.

We all live in a comfortable rut.

If you can remember the 60's you really weren't there.

I have all these pictures. It looks like all leather and hair. Who owns this dog?

Thirty percent of the people in the world eat with chopsticks. Thirty percent eat with a knife, fork and spoon. Thirty percent eat with their hands. The other ten percent don't have any food.

Do you know what a Pebble Beach woman is? She has an impeccable tan, plays golf every day and thinks tipping is a city in China.

Do you know what's nice about being Chinese? I can't think of anything.

How do the Chinese name their children? Throw a spoon on the floor.

A homeless man told a Pebble Beach woman he hadn't had a bite to eat in four days. She said, "God, I admire your will power."

Why do women rub their eyes when they wake up in the morning? They don't have any balls to scratch.

Why didn't God give women any brains? He didn't give them a dick to carry them in.

If God is love, and love is blind, is Ray Charles God?

What is endless love? Ray Charles and Stevie Wonder playing tennis.

What do you call a black man being chased by 20 white men across a golf course? Tiger Woods.

Tigers have stripes leopards have spots.

Don't trust the poppin' fresh doughboy. He is too happy for someone without a dick.

Buckwheat has embraced Islam. He is now known as Kahreem O Wheat.

Nothing can be made any worse by saying it out loud.

He, who travels alone, travels fastest.

If you take your friends with you, you won't have anyone to come home to.

If I knew then what I know now I still wouldn't have had the money.

You are more creative on an empty stomach.

Why doesn't Tarzan have a beard?

What is the difference between monkeys and apes? Monkeys have tails.

This job is like the monkey's tail. Someday it will all be behind me.

What did the monkey say when he got his tail cut off? It won't be long now.

I have been thrown out of better bars than this one.

I don't hang out in bars, just this one.

She was bred in old Kentucky, but she is just a crumb up here.

Do you know why they took the 911 numbers off the Honolulu police cars? The Samoans were stealing them. They thought they were Porsches.

Elvis was the King of Rock and Roll. He died on the throne.

Elvis had meat loaf and mashed potatoes for dinner every night for a year. It's the sign of an addictive personality.

Don't let your meat loaf.

Don't take any wooden pulses.

Have a good year.

The difference between a used tire casing and 100 used condoms? One is a Goodyear one is a great year.

Have a nice life and a mellow afterwards.

I will see you around, if you don't go square.

Get out of my dreams and get back to work.

Why don't you tell your dreams to me? Your fantasies will set you free.

If you don't have a dream, how can a dream come true?

When you dream you create.

The worst people are the ones who prey on your mind.

You only think you are bad, until somebody bad has you for breakfast.

We had the preacher for Sunday dinner. We passed him around and cut him up.

A woman's place is in the home, and she should report there immediately after work.

The first hour of the morning is the rudder for the day.

It's the first Fredrico in the morning I love.

You can't have everything. Where would you keep it?

When you feel bad because you don't get the things you want, feel good because you don't get the things you don't want.

Be careful what you ask for. You may get it.

If you don't ask, you don't get.

If you line everybody up and tell them something, two percent will not get the word.

Two percent of the people will take up 98% of your time.

In every load of ducks there is a turkey.

The only time she says, "No" is when I ask if she's had enough.

There is a lot of truth in a jest.

Comedy is when you take the truth and add a curlicue on the end.

Some guys only laugh when you walk into the tongue on their boat trailer.

Humor comes through a door you didn't know you left open.

If you die doing stand up comedy in Siberia, do you get hit with frozen tomatoes?

Stroke me gently.

You can't go wrong gouging the rich.

We are so rich we are stinking.

Don't hang out with the rich; they never pay.

Throw your big leg over me momma; it may not feel this good again.

The harder I work the luckier I get.

At these prices this ought to be the best food you have ever had.

Anytime the food is artfully arranged on the plate, the chef has had his hands all over it.

The last time I went out to dinner, the waiter walked up to the table and I said, "Do you know you have your thumb on my steak?"

He said, "Yeah, I didn't want to drop it again."

I asked the waiter for iodine, but iodined alone.

Waiter, what is this green stuff on my plate? "It's either very new cheese or very old meat."

They use a lot of Tabasco in the islands to pass old meat.

We have been together so long we are on our second bottle of Tabasco.

Why does my almond have legs?

What is this fly doing in my soup? "It looks like it's drowning."

They outlawed asbestos but we do asbestos we can.

Not the best, but hard to beat.

The best is the enemy of the good.

When I'm good I'm good. When I'm bad I'm better.

Stick with something you are good at.

God knows where that glove has been.

Enzymes are the secret to life.

Why do the French line their streets with trees? So the Germans can march in the shade.

The bigger the German the smaller the bikini.

The bigger the German the louder he will order drinks from someone who doesn't speak the language.

Body by Nautilus, mind by Mattel.

How do you catch a unique rabbit? You neak up on it.

How do you catch a tame rabbit? Tame way.

What does the Easter Bunny get for making a basket? Two points, the same as everyone else.

Would you take me off your list of people to call?

We like to freeze paint balls and shoot them at the neighbor kids.

You play by ear. I sing through my nose by ear.

You're OK. I will work on it.

I never signed on as OK.

I gave a speech; there wasn't a dry seat in the house.

What a critic. You should write a column.

My favorite medium is a spray can and a bridge.

We all suffer for our art.

To women over 40, lower your standards.

Romantic love is when you make love with a feather. Kinky is when you use the whole chicken.

The ability to accessorize separates us from the lower animals.

The best clothes attract the least attention.

In the long run the best is the cheapest.

Good clothes open all doors.

Beware of any job that requires new clothes.

He knows the water best that has waded through it.

I don't drink water, fish screw in it.

My drinks make you thirsty.

A little boy asked his father the difference between ignorance and apathy? He said, "I don't know and I don't care."

If cute were in, Winnie the Pooh would be playing Las Vegas.

Sometimes in life you have to ask yourself, "What would the Lone Ranger do?"

Sometimes you ask yourself, "What would I tell a board of inquiry?"

I used to talk to myself but I got too many wrong answers.

Why does a fart smell? For the benefit of those who can't hear.

A coon smells his own tracks first.

A pedigree never treed a coon.

The best thing I make is tracks out of here.

If it looks like I am getting smaller it's because I am leaving.

Make like a tree and leaf.

Don't go away mad, just go away.

You only go around once in life, you better learn to embezzle.

Flattery is soft soap and soft soap is 90% lye.

My brother is an only child.

It's been nice having you. I hope you've enjoyed being had.

It's been nice taking you around. I hope you've enjoyed being taken.

You have a point there. Put a hat on it and nobody will notice.

It must have slipped out I don't think anybody heard.

If athletes get athlete's foot, what do astronauts get? Missile toe.

What kind of music do aliens listen to? Neptunes.

Do not turn the gravity on to awaken the crew.

Do not send a hologram of yourself on a blind date.

There are no passengers on space ship earth we are all crew.

Floggings will continue until morale improves.

The more you have to do the more time you find to do it in.

What do you call a musician without a girl friend? Homeless.

What you call a guy who hangs out with musicians? Drummer.

What is another name for the drummer? Roady.

Did you hear about Alexander Grahamski? The first telephone Pole.

There are more termites on this planet than any other living thing. If all the termites were divided up all the people would get 15 pounds.

What's a termite's favorite vegetable? Lattice.

Did you hear about the toothless termite that walked into a bar? He asked, "Where is the bar tender?"

For sheer numbers the algae in the ocean are the most numerous things on the planet.

The number of things that can fly, on this planet, is an indication that flying is nature's preferred way of getting around.

If we were meant to fly, we would have been born with landing lights.

I just flew in from the coast and are my arms tired.

Flying is no big deal; bugs do it.

Helicopters are an assault on machinery to defy gravity.

Gravity will get you down.

If it's not broke, fix it until it is.

When all is said and done, more will be said than done.

If you're like me, and I know I am.

A wild goose is a half-inch off center.

If Daddy gets drunk, Momma gets mad. If Momma gets drunk, Daddy doesn't know.

I like old ladies who slam down an empty martini glass before you can write out a check, and ask for a room number, and say, "This will be cash, Sonny."

What do you do if you are standing on a street corner and your toe falls off? You call a toe truck.

The last time I saw a leg that bad it had a toe tag on it.

You can't get there from here; you have to go down town first.

I remember when she told me where to go.

Free advice is worth what you pay for it.

There is no such thing as a free Willy.

This too shall pass.

You work harder as a role model.

You know how these things work.

There is nothing as corrosive as salt water. It never stops moving.

The natives say, "Everything dies but the ocean. The ocean never remembers."

When you are fighting the jungle out your front door, it is coming through your back window.

Any plant out of place is a weed. I don't love plants. I hate weeds.

He was a worldly man, bigger at the equator than the poles.

If you put all the lawyers head-to-toe at the equator, that would be good.

What do you say to a lawyer with an IQ of 70? Good morning your honor.

The only justice in the halls of justice is in the halls.

What this world needs is a judge that will stay bribed.

You can cure an ice cream headache by drinking warm water.

You can cure hiccups by sucking on a lime with a few drops of Angostura bitters on it.

You can stop the hiccups by rubbing your ear lobe.

You can stifle a sneeze by rubbing the end of your nose.

You can control nausea by pinching the web between your thumb and forefinger.

Why are they called apartments when they are so close together?

Why is it called a highway when it is down on the ground?

Why is there such a difference between a day off and an off day?

Why is a slim chance and a fat chance the same thing?

Why is there such a difference between a wise man and a wise guy?

Why is it called cargo on a ship and shipment in a car?

Why do we drive on parkways and park on driveways?

What are the first three words in an Armenian cookbook? Steal a pig.

Why do Armenian names end in ian? I'm all nose.

She had a Roman nose. It roamed all over her face.

Hawaii is changing and not for the better.

Kick a rock.

I asked her to come home with me. She said, "Is there room under your rock?"

Call the chaplain he likes everybody.

A bartender lands a part in a local play. He has one line. "Hark the cannon roars." Since he works nights he can't go to play practice. But, he practices his line, "Hark the cannon roars, and hark the cannon roars." He says it softly, loudly, says it high and low. He misses the dress rehearsal, but the first night the play is on he gets off early, and runs down to the theater. The director cues him. He runs onto the stage and hears a tremendous BOOM and yells, "What in the hell was that?"

Always have another line ready. It's like playing tennis. Most people have a good shot or two, but they don't know what to do if the ball keeps coming back.

Two cats are watching a tennis game. Their heads are following the ball back and forth. One asks, "Do you really like this game?"

The other replies, "My father is in the racket."

Look out for number one, but don't step in number two.

What is the last thing you take off before going to bed? You take your feet off the floor.

What is the definition of a gentleman? Someone who can play the accordion and doesn't.

A gentleman never hurries, is never late, and never pays.

A gentleman does nothing, and everything is done for him.

What is an optimist? A banjo player with a beeper.

An intellectual is someone who can listen to the William Tell overture and not think of the Lone Ranger.

Once a King always a King. Once a night's enough.

Help me with these bags. I'll get the blonde you get the redhead.

Another day and another dollar for the union.

The last kid I gave two cherries to threw them on the ground and yelled, "Stop staring at me."

The mind loves routine.

The more you change your mind the cleaner it will be.

Anytime there is a confrontation between the will and the imagination, the imagination wins out.

What's the difference between your wife and your job? After three years your job still sucks.

I have CRS syndrome. I can't remember shit.

Physically you are what you eat. Mentally you are what you think. Spiritually you are what you believe. Really you are a clump of mud that rose up and walks around. You will turn back into dust and be blown away by the cosmic wind. It makes you wonder what comes in, on the wind. Who was this dust?

A clean desk is the sign of a sick mind.

The job isn't done until you leave some blood on it.

A massage is a beating you pay for.

An Englishman is never at home unless he is abroad.

Why is six afraid of seven? Because seven ate nine.

You won't have a headache on the sixth if you don't buy a fifth on the fourth.

Your chances of winning the lottery are the same whether you play it or not.

A man understands life when he begins to plant trees in whose shade he will never sit.

Do you know what your navel is for? To hold salt when you eat celery in bed.

Nothing ventured, accomplished same.

When in doubt make it stout.

BENITO

He was laughing so hard, hitting the hood of his truck that he was throwing up. That's why I did it. To give Benito the good laugh.

He had arranged this contest with a rival gang, on the railroad. I beat the competition so bad it was funny, and Benito took all their money. They were a bunch of blowhards who needed a lesson in humility.

We were on a stretch of track just out of town. The race was pulling spikes, between two red flags. I was a ringer. The man I beat was a friendly cuss. He started out strong using his hammer and aligning bar to lift each spike and pull it out. An aligning bar is used to align the track, after it is gauged. It is a piece of solid steel, five feet long, one and one-half inch in diameter, and heavy. There is a claw at the foot. He placed this claw against the spike and hit the heel of the bar with a sledgehammer to home it in for the pull. He didn't have any tricks up his sleeve. He just knew how to work.

The joints are staggered. He led, so was out of the way. He was on one rail and I on the other. He would pull the two outside spikes, then cross the rail, like a gandy dancer, to pull the inner two. The crews were lined up on both sides of the track, cheering. It was late in the day, in the Panhandle of Oklahoma. Lightning forked over the hills on the horizon. Electricity was in the air.

At the halfway point, I went to work. Dropping the hammer and turning the bar over revealed a chisel point. He hadn't noticed because it had been covered with a glove. I shoved the giant screwdriver under the plate and lifted all four spikes at once. I pulled them out with one hand. These were old ties and the spikes had been there for 50 years. I ran down the track to the next joint, used the same technique and pulled those spikes, and the next, and the next, and made it to the finish flag before the challenger would believe what he was seeing. I walked down the hill laughing, and gave Benito a hand.

Benito was our foreman. He was Cherokee, and tanned colonial oak. He always wore blue overalls, a white shirt and a white hard-hat, with cowboy boots. He was short, had a shock of white hair, looked 80 and must have been 40 years old. He was thin-boned and gaunt. He reminded me of someone who had escaped from a concentration camp.

There were ten of us in the extra gang. We were hired to change the joints on a spur of track between Boise City, Oklahoma and Las Animas, Colorado. We lived on a train. There was a sleeping car, a tool car and a water car, parked on a side track at the depot in Boise City. Half of the group were kids new to the job. Half were hardened railroad types and a mean bunch. My father warned me not to take this job.

We started out pulling spikes, all ten of us. It took us a week to do a mile of track. Benito watched us, and picked the players on his team. I went through the tool car looking at all the aligning bars. Not all tools are created equal. I found the one with the chisel end, and the thin-toed claw. It seemed to be made of sterner stuff than the rest. Using it meant a boot kick would do the trick. I didn't have to carry a hammer. If a kick wouldn't do it, then jamming the chisel end under the rail and lifting would.

We had two machines that were gas-powered to remove the bolts. One man held a tool while the other held a large socket on the nut and gave it the gas. All they did was remove bolts and move on. Two more men knocked off the old joints and the old tie plate. One man greased. He had a five-gallon can of black goo and a big brush. He hit both sides of the rail. The same two workmen placed the new joints in position with a new tie-plate and started the nuts on the bolts. One was inside the rail one was outside.

The second machine tightened the bolts. The last man drove the spikes. He used a spike mall. It has enough meat to miss the rail and let you drive from either side. He put four spikes in each plate.

We took turns running the machines, and doing each job. Benito watched. I broke so many spike mall handles that Benito brought in a whole carload. We were the laughingstock of Santa Fe. He wouldn't let me near a hammer.

He put me to pulling spikes. I pulled every joint spike between those little towns. We started doing a mile of track a day.

We rode to work on a motorcar that pulled a trailer with our tools from the depot to the work site. There were levers stored in holsters we used to roll the vehicles off on a siding. Benito would set a sign at the start and another sign a mile down the track. I would start pulling spikes and in a few minutes be away from the noise and grease. It was clean. I'd pull the spikes out of the joints on the left and then the right and just walk down the track. I would stop at the sign and look for artifacts, until Benito came for lunch.

This part of the Santa Fe rail followed the Santa Fe Trail, right into Bent's Fort, along the Arkansas River. Wagon ruts from a hundred years ago mark the prairie. There was lots of stuff scattered around way off the road, where no one ever goes. There are many unmarked graves. You never forgot you were walking over the bones of those who had come before.

On the ride back, I would place a can of food on the exhaust manifold of the four-cylinder engine, and have a hot lunch with the gang. Benito always had the same lunch, a bottle of Seagram's V.O. whiskey and a can of hot chili peppers. After lunch I would help with other things until the day was done. Then we would go drinking.

The county we were in had private clubs. There were no open bars. You had to be a member, take your own bottle and they would sell you a set-up. You made your drink at the table. Benito would wear his white hard-hat, knock on the door and say, "Santa Fe" and they would let us in. We would drink until they closed, then drive back to the train and go to sleep. We kept our cars at the depot. All of us went somewhere on weekends.

I had a girlfriend in Texas, one in Colorado and one in town. The girl in Colorado was an enigma. I had been trying for two quarters at a Junior College to get into her knickers. She called me on a Friday night, after I had worked all day on the rails, and driven 150 miles home. I had just showered, finished dinner, and was sitting down to watch TV with my father.

She said, "I am all alone. My mother and stepfather are gone to a family reunion in Lamar. You want to come see me?"

I gazed out the window at my blue Oldsmobile, full of gas. A front was moving in and snow was beginning to fall. It was 200 miles to where she lived. I knew a back road, across the plains, where the cops seldom go.

"I'll be there in two hours," I said and hung up.

The car's speedometer was a ribbon that changed from yellow, to orange, to red. When it was pegged it turned white. I kept it in the white, and the lights on bright, and was early.

But it was late for a date. We exchanged pleasantries and hit the sack. It wasn't the first time for either of us, just the first time together. I slept like a drugged man for two hours when she shook me awake and whispered, "My parents are here!" It was an L-shaped house. I pulled open the curtain and sure enough the drunken stepfather was standing atop the stairs at the back door, and beating on it. He had offended the relatives at the reunion and they ran him off. He was a jerk when sober. I didn't want to deal with him drunk.

I looked down and saw the mother, with her hands cupped around her face, looking in the bedroom window. She was staring at my man-hood, looking for the daughter, and couldn't comprehend why she couldn't see into the room.

I had a bomber jacket with my socks and shorts stuffed in one pocket, and my shirt in the other. It was rolled with my Levi's on the couch, next to the front door. I stepped into my shoes barefoot and picked up my clothes on the way out. I dressed on the front steps, pulling on my pants and jacket. Then I slipped across their front yard.

It had stopped snowing. There was three inches on the ground, and it was cold. I jumped the fence into the neighbor's yard and hit a patch of ice and went down into a swing set. While fighting chains and swing seats I heard the dog. A giant German shepherd came bounding down the porch, barked, and headed for me. He hit a patch of ice and in his excitement just ran in place. I crept across the ice, eyeing the dog, and stepped over a chain link fence and into the alley.

She lived across from a motel. I ran down the alley and came around the front to the office. I burst in, turned on the light, rang the bell and hit the buzzer. The clock behind the counter read

3:00 a.m. A fat lady in curlers and a robe came from the back. I handed her $35 and said, "I need a room please."

She looked at me, barely dressed, hair a mess, covered with lipstick and marinated in aftershave and perfume, and asked, "Any luggage?"

"No, just what's on me."

She took the money and handed me a card. While I was registering she found a key and said, "Number 17, all the way down to the end."

The room was right across from her house. I could hear her stepfather calling her names. Her mother was yelling at them both. The poor girl was screaming to defend herself. All the lights were on, and all hell was breaking loose. I called the police and told them the truth.

When the dispatcher answered, I said. "I have been working on the railroad all day. I am down here in the local motel, and the people in the house across from me are having some kind of a party, and I can't get any sleep."

The dispatcher said, "We will take care of it. Thank you for calling." I turned off the light, opened the curtains and waited. In five minutes a police car crunched up her driveway. Two officers approached the door. They told the stepfather to turn out the lights and knock off the noise. "We've had complaints."

We all went to sleep. I awoke at the crack of noon. I took my time getting dressed, then walked over to her house. She was the only one up. We went for a ride. It was the sweetest afternoon talking about it, and trying to figure out what to do. I took her home around sunset. Her mother and stepfather were at the kitchen table. They were in bathrobes, hung over, having coffee and cigarettes, and staring at their food. They didn't have much to say, and didn't say much. My point of view was, "It's mind over matter. If you don't mind. It doesn't matter."

When I arrived at the depot the following Monday morning, the gang was gathered around a trash barrel, warming their hands on the fire. Benito was there. I told them about my escape, and then asked Benito, "What would you have done if you would have caught me with your daughter?"

He said, "I don't know. Let me think about it. I will tell you later."

I was out in front all morning and didn't see him until noon. He didn't say anything about it, but I could tell he was thinking. After lunch, and his log entry, he stayed in his truck. He stared out the window, smoked, and stroked his chin.

That evening while I was sitting on my bunk, and writing to the girl in Texas, Benito stopped by and said, "I figured out what I would do, if it was you."

"Yes?"

"I would hand you a 20-dollar bill and say, go buy yourself a good piece of ass, and leave her alone." I admire Benito's particular way of dealing with people.

One night Benito and I were in the depot at Boise City, visiting with the agent. He worked nights and manned the telegraph key. He collected Edsels. He had three of those things and loved them. He would drive one to work. He seemed to be forever working on the wiring harness in the middle of the steering wheel that controlled the entire car.

We had V.O. in a paper sack. It was Benito's calling card. It was late, and we were telling jokes and laughing. There wasn't any action on the telegraph key, and we really didn't hear the fellow walk in. He was just standing there looking at us.

He looked like he had been used to sweep the street. He was dirty, mud-caked, bloody and torn. Benito, ever the diplomat, asked, "Jesus Christ, buddy, what happened to you?" He related how he had lost everything: his wife, job, family and all his money. He had tried to commit suicide by jumping from a train, doing about 70 miles an hour. He hit a bunch of tumbleweeds in the ditch and just got scratched up coming to a stop.

The agent asked, "Do you want us to get you some help? Would you like a ride somewhere? How about a drink?" He nodded and indicated Benito's sack. He refused any assistance and asked how many blocks it was to town, and left.

Benito said "Poor bastard" and the lights went out. We talked about life's problems in the dark and then a police car and a fire truck pulled up. They were shining a light on the high-voltage poles next to the depot. We went out and looked. The man had climbed a pole and grabbed the wires. He was one with the grid.

The train was moved to Campo, Colorado. Campo is one cafe and 17 churches in the sand dunes, left over from the dust bowl days. The ranchers bring their families to church on Sunday and Campo fills up. There is no bar. We had to drive to drink, either to Boise City, or Springfield, Colorado; some nights both.

We were in the bar in Springfield one evening, in a back booth. The old-gal bartender had taken a shine to me. She came and dragged me out of my seat and pushed me into the back room. She asked, "You see those cases of beer on the floor?" I did. She said, "Stack them on these shelves and if anybody comes in here, don't talk to them." I was putting the last one on the shelf, when a man stuck his head through the door and nodded at me. He closed the door without saying anything. I put all the beer back on the floor and then on the shelf again.

The bartender finally came and rescued me. She said, "You almost met the Liquor Inspector. How old are you anyway?"

"Nineteen."

In Springfield I was hit with a bullwhip. My buddy Al and I were dating the waitresses in the local cafe. The gentleman who owned the cafe is an artist. His watercolor prints cover one wall. He sold enough paintings to keep the place open as a public service. He was gone for the day, and the girls were closing. The restaurant was decorated in a western motif with wagon wheels on the walls, cowbells, old guns, harnesses, etc. Al took a bullwhip down and was cracking it in the room. We were the only ones there. A kid at my school had lost an eye messing with a whip. I cautioned, "Be careful with that thing."

He turned and cracked it at me. The little leather piece on the end was going super-sonic when it touched my left calf. Damn that hurt. It felt the same as when the leg was sprayed with mace, and cut with a razor. It was a good thing I was sitting at the counter, or I would have fallen. It took an hour for the pain to go away. It left a little red mark that was sore the next day. Al was apologetic enough. It was damn little consolation for the pain he inflicted.

One morning an elk made the mistake of walking past the train. A rifle shot rang out and the beast fell over. A Mexican who worked with us was out there with his rifle still smoking, skinning the thing. The carcass steamed in the morning chill. He had a large family and took the meat home. He gave Benito the heart. I can still remember elk heart and chili peppers fried in V.O. for breakfast. After the third plate, it is so smooth. Benito was running around in his long johns and socks cooking over a Coleman stove in an iron skillet. Cigarette ashes almost fell in every time he moved.

Life was good. We had extension cords to the depot for our stereo and lights. There were Coleman stoves and ice chests. For a time we had a car full of ice. It was insulated and filled with 300-pound blocks. There were stairs for access. The money was good. The work was hard and dangerous. There were bunk beds in the car and cabinets for our gear.

One night a locomotive hooked onto us and yanked us to a wreck sight. One minute we're sleeping, the next we we're flying down the track and our stuff was falling on our heads. Our cords were torn away from the depot and dragging behind us. There's no light and every man is cussing the dark amidst the general confusion of a submarine going down. Benito slept through it all. The only way he knew we were moved is when he woke up to take a piss and fell out the door into a snow bank. "Hey! What asshole took the stairs?" he yelled.

Right before the Cimarron river bridge, eight cars, full of lard, jumped the track and tore up 1400 ties. The trucks cut them in half. The train was gone by the time we were there and the next day we began replacing the ties. A work train came in loaded with tools, rails, and hundreds of ties. A burrow crane began off-loading the ties. They were strapped on each end with steel tape, sixteen to a bundle.

I was down in a fill area answering nature's call. The crane swung a bundle of ties over my head. The hook was on a piece of chain that ran through the two steel bands. I looked up and one of the bands broke. The bundle of ties was being carried horizontally. The crane operator stopped the boom. The bundle fell vertical and motionless about 40 feet overhead. One of the ties fell from the bundle and the rest fanned out and fell all around me. Benito yelled, "You are the luckiest guy I have ever met. Now bring all of them up here."

A new railroad tie has been soaking in creosote for two years. It is eight inches square and eight feet long, and weighs over two hundred pounds. Two men use tongs to lift one. I threw one over each shoulder and walked up the hill. I made eight trips. It is the hardest thing I have ever done. My heart was pounding in my ears; my vision doubled, and my core temperature was too high. It made the right impression, and established my place in the pecking order. No man messed with me after that.

The ties we removed were supposed to be saved for the railroad. The worst ones were. The best ones Benito had stacked out of sight and sold to the local farmers for fence post. The money we spent drinking. When all the ties were replaced we had fits finding the right amount of rail. It would break at night and go serpentine in the afternoon heat.

"Never sit on a joint" is Benito's rule. It can slam shut and take a chunk out of your ass. The rails expand during the day and contract at night. The joints have a gap in the morning. The gap closes as the day warms up. You can hear them snapping in the heat. We had the disadvantage of a downgrade. Gravity assisted the expansion, and resisted the contraction.

Each time we changed the length, we had to align it. Benito would stand up the track and sight, while the gang stood ready. We were five inside the rails and five out, all facing the same way. We shouldered our aligning bars and shoved them under the rails. Someone would count to three and then we would heave in the direction Benito was pointing. When he pointed straight up, that section was in line and we moved to another area and did it again. This is the hardest work you can imagine. To experience this agony, put your shoulder against the corner of a building and push it over. When the wreck sight was repaired, the train was moved to Springfield and we picked up where we left off.

Some of the guys carried handguns. One morning, while riding to work on the trailer, a guy pulled a .357 pistol, held it next to my ear, and shot a sign along side the track. The noise was deafening. I yelled, "What the hell do you think you are doing?"

"I was trying to hit that sign."

"You don't need a gun to hit those signs." I grabbed one of the bolts we used in the joints. It's an inch in diameter and four inches long. I hurled it at the next sign we passed. It ricocheted and returned, hitting the gunman's hard-hat. Now he was pissed. The bolt pierced the helmet and ran alongside the sweatband without breaking the skin. Benito stopped the car, came back and told us to cool it.

"Save your bullets for snakes," he advised.

Taking point, I worked my way into a curve on high ground. I banged a plate on the outside of the rail. As the hammer hit, a rattlesnake bit the handle. The fangs extended and venom shot out. I nailed it in the head with the aligning bar and threw it on the side. I kept pulling spikes and finding more serpents. Eight snakes were stacked when Benito came for lunch.

He looked at the pile and grinned, and danced around them, "I told you there would be snakes up here. They always come in here after a rain." Getting bit by a snake on the railroad is considered dereliction of duty, and it will cost you your job. We had heard the story about the man trying to catch a snake and was bitten in the attempt. He doesn't work here any more.

As we closed on the main line, the train was moved to Las Animas. My family had a ranch not far from there so I started commuting. Benito and I would car-pool to the work site. Some bars in Colorado open at 6:00 a.m., and serve food. I would meet Benito in one for breakfast. He would have a beer. I would order him an omelet, along with my food. When it came he would ask, "What's this?"

"That's food. You have to eat if you are going to last forever. You know what my Uncle Jake says, 'You have to get something in you to make a turd.'"

He would eat a few bites, push it away and light a cigarette. I would frown at him as he took a drink of beer. He would smile and say, "You're all right, Chung." It was his Indian name for me. It meant bodyguard and bait.

It was after one of these meals that the Road master and the Division Engineer were waiting for us along side the track. Benito said, "Oh oh," as we pulled up. He reached into his glove box and took out a large white onion. He bit off a chunk, to hide the beer on his breath, and walked over to them chewing, and tearing. The Road master was a handful but the Division Engineer was my buddy.

He taught me how to make margaritas. We would buy all the lemons in town, and then roll them on his kitchen table to break the pulp. We mixed the lemon juice with equal parts Tequila and Triple Sec in a Thermos, and took it to the airport. There was a dirt strip south of town. We would rent a tail-dragger and practice crosswind landings, under power. The plane had tandem seats. I would sit behind him and hold the Thermos. He would do touch-and-goes, and laugh. He was okay.

Benito stood downwind and chain-smoked while they talked. They told him the train was being moved back to Oklahoma and we were to begin replacing the joints going the other way.

We were in the lobby of the Crystal Hotel in Boise City watching TV. It was Tommy Smothers who said, "Anyone would have to be crazy to volunteer to be a Corpsman in Viet Nam." I had a reputation for doing crazy things in those days, so I went down to the Navy Recruiter and signed up. I was drafted the next day. It didn't matter anyway. Benito said I was crazy.

The last time I saw him, he shook my hand and said, "I won't see you in this life again." I thought what a strange thing for him to say. Three weeks later he was caught in bed with an old gal. Her husband shot them both.

NEEDLES

The Security Chief at Oak Knoll was a mean motor scooter and a bad go-getter. He busted two of my roommates out of the Navy, for being crazy. He put the third one behind bars in the brig and he was after me. I was running out of guys to hang out with, and because of him I became a 4.0 sailor. He held weekly inspections. My shoes were always shined; my hair was cut; I never needed a shave; my clothes were always clean and I saluted everything that moved and painted everything that didn't. He would go over us with a fine-tooth comb, looking for a thread that was out of place. He never found anything on me.

For a deputy he had a fat, sadistic, First Class Petty Officer, who carried a clipboard and kept track of everything. He was easy to confuse, but the Chief was nobody's fool. When the Chief went home, the First cruised alone.

In the wee hours of a morning, when I was working the graveyard shift in the emergency room, those two showed up. The First was carrying the Chief. They both reeked of booze. I put him on a bed and closed the curtain. The Chief had two puncture wounds on the top of his head. The cuts were one-half inch wide, an inch long, and about one-quarter inch apart.

"What happened to him?" I inquired.

"He fell and hit a locker," said the First.

"Was the locker carrying a claw-hammer? That looks like what got him. Either that or someone buried the ugly end of a crowbar in his head."

The First ushered me across the room. He whispered, "We just want you to sew him up. Don't say anything about this, and don't make an entry in his Health Record."

I took exception to this. "What if he has a concussion, or brain damage? You should at least get an X-ray, and if he worsens you damn sure want an entry in his Health Record."

"Don't give us any shit. Just do like we tell you and keep your mouth shut."

I sewed up the Chief, and did the best job I could. I cleaned the scalp but didn't shave it. I irrigated with a local anesthetic, but didn't inject to keep the swelling down. If he felt anything, he didn't complain. I pushed back the hairs and slowly pulled the edges of the wounds together. I used sutures that matched his hair color and didn't bandage it. When he left, under his own power, you couldn't tell he had been hit.

From then on, at inspections the Chief would look the other way. I was still squared away, but I could have been nude, and it wouldn't have mattered. When I walked off the base, rather than being searched I was just waved through. When my room in the barracks was inspected, he just poked his head in the door.

One afternoon I came to my room and there were four Hospital Corpsmen I didn't know. They didn't introduce themselves, just said they had something they wanted to talk to me about.

"So let's talk."

"Not here," said the senior one. "We want you to go for a ride with us."

"I don't know about that."

"You won't be harmed. If you are not interested in helping us you will be returned here. We are shipmates and we are all in the same boat."

"May I ask where we are going?"

"To an apartment building in Oakland."

We walked outside to a gray Navy truck filled with furniture. There were beds, chairs, tables, trash cans, dressers, night stands, lamps, springs, bedding, curtains, silverware, china and blankets piled on the truck. Three of them crawled in the cab. The other helped me up in the back. We drove to the gate. The First rushed out clutching his clipboard. He had an evil grin on his face. He looked up and saw me, and froze. He stepped back on his island and waved us through.

We drove to an apartment building surrounded by other buildings that looked just the same. The five of us hustled the furniture into a three-bedroom unit on the second floor. One guy wiped off the kitchen table; another produced a coffee machine and made a pot. We pulled up a chair and had a cup.

The leader explained that they worked on the orthopedic wards with the Naval Prosthetics Research Laboratory. They rehabilitated the long-term patients--the ones with traumatic amputations who were waiting for artificial limbs. There was a lot of physical therapy, a lot of fitting, and a lot of pain. "These guys have been shunned by their families. Their girlfriends or wives aren't interested in them anymore. Many are depressed, despondent and suicidal. Some are just waiting, and use morphine as an escape. We would rather see them smoking non-narcotic marijuana."

Then he explained how they traded needles to heroin addicts for the grass. The needles went out one way and the grass came in another. "Isn't that risky letting the patients smoke on the wards?" I asked.

"If we can bring them to places like this it is safer. If they can't travel we roll them outside and downwind."

"How do you decide who gets to smoke?"

"We make it available to all. We don't force it on anyone; we don't deny anyone; and we don't charge anyone. We consider the needles going out Navy property and the pot coming in Navy property. We are just exchanging one for another."

"Why do you do this?"

"It is not something we started. It is something we inherited, and we consider it a conscious effort to help our fellow man." The rest of them shook their heads in agreement.

"How can I help you?"

"We have noticed that you are not hassled when you go past the security shack. We notice you are invisible at inspections. We have heard they do not search your room. You seem to operate with impunity where security is concerned."

"I stay squared away and keep my act together."

"Maybe so, maybe not. Anyway, today was a test and you passed with flying colors."

"How is that?" I asked.

"The truck and all this furniture are stolen. We thought if you can take this much off base, there should be no problem with a little, black backpack. All we want you to do is carry a backpack off base once a week and deliver it to this address on Haight Street, in San Francisco." He handed me a card with a lettered street address.

"What is in it for me?"

He looked exhausted but remained composed. He continued, "This is a felonious pursuit, the punishment for which can only be compounded by profit. There is nothing in it for you, and there is nothing in it for us. No money enters this equation."

"Why should I bother?"

"To lessen the risk for us all. You haven't gone to Viet Nam yet. You may come back and occupy one of those beds. Wouldn't you like a choice?"

"I will have to think about this." They drove me back. The First waved the empty truck through the gate. They dropped me off at the barracks and I never saw them again.

A week later I walked into my room and there was a black backpack on a chair. I hefted it and felt three long boxes of 16-gauge needles. I thought, "What the Hell," and put it on. I walked out the gate without a second look from anybody. I kicked the motorcycle to life and glanced up at the freeway. It was bumper-to-bumper traffic all the way. I split the lane up the ramp and rode between the stopped cars like they weren't there.

I found the address on Haight Street and walked in. It was a hippie shooting gallery. There were posters on the walls, with blankets hanging between them. Strings of beads barred the doorframes. There was no furniture, just cushions and carpets. Men and women were sprawled around. Weird music was playing. It stank of incense, pot smoke and Ajax cleanser. Two hippies were arguing over how to transport LSD to Mexico in the hubcap of a VW Microbus.

One furry freak brother rose up and noticed me holding the backpack. He spoke, "Just set it over there man." He pointed at a spool for cable used as a table. I set it down, and left. I walked past a hippie on the sidewalk selling blocks of C4 plastique explosive. He made the media the next day.

The trips became a routine. Every week or two the backpack would be in my room. I would take it over, and began doing sick call on the addicts. I would check their vital signs and listen to their problems. I warned them about becoming dehydrated, and begged them to eat. I soon learned not to take any money with me. Heroin addicts are consummate beggars. If you have $100 on you they will get it before you leave. If you have 14-

cents in your pocket they want it. I would lock my wallet in the battery box of the bike.

I would make coffee for them. You use one scoop of instant coffee and 16 scoops sugar. I considered the needles someone else's doing. I was just making coffee, for the heroin addicts, as a public service.

THE BRIDGE

There is a bar on the Bay Bridge. Oh, yes there is. It's a piece of pipe about eight inches in diameter. It parallels the span at a little over four feet high. You can watch it out the window of your car as you drive by. It bars you from jumping, or throwing anything over the side. It will control your car, and keep it from going in the ocean. There is a sidewalk between the bar and the roadway. I had the front wheel of a motorcycle over this pipe and was straining to lift the rear wheel. The San Francisco police stopped in a blue-and-white car with lights flashing. We had a chat.

It was midnight Halloween, 1968. I was heading home from a party in Oakland, after consuming several beers, and a gallon of wine. The day had been spent in bittersweet revelry. We were saying good-bye to nurses we had worked with for a year, and to corpsmen who were going to Viet Nam. Each of us realized we might not see the other again. We drank, sang songs, made love, told stories, hugged and kissed good-bye. They stood under the porch light waving as I kicked life into the bike and rode away. There was no electric starter.

Home was a cot in a room with three other guys on Treasure Island. A man-made island, build for the 1920 World's Fair. We were assigned to the Marines and waiting on orders. The Navy supplied the Marine Corps with Hospital Corpsmen, Doctors and Chaplains. After two years training to be a Field Service Medical Technician, a change was coming.

Alcohol has never been my ally; it is more my enemy. It leaves you breathless, and I was panting like a road lizard when they started yelling at me.

"PUT THAT MOTORCYCLE DOWN ON THE SIDEWALK, AND PUT YOUR HANDS IN THE AIR," came over the loudspeaker on top of the car. They had the windows rolled up and the doors locked. A pump shotgun hung over the seat, on a partition of diamond-wire with a Plexiglas back.

Leaving the motorcycle where it was and walking over to the car, I yelled, "You guys get out of there and give me a hand. This thing is heavy."

"YOU CANNOT THROW IT OFF THE BRIDGE."

"Why not? It ain't gonna hurt nobody. Then you can give me a ticket for hitch-hiking," I slurred. "I want to donate this piece-of-junk to the Bay Area."

I had worked on this motorcycle full time for a year, just to ride it part time. It was worn out when I bought it, used, and it cost more to keep running than payments would have been on new one. Its name was Max. I was fatalistic and leaving the country, and probably not coming back. I was having a throwing away party and here was help.

"IF YOU THROW IT OFF THE BRIDGE YOU HAVE TO PAY TO HAVE IT DREDGED UP TO MAKE SURE THERE IS NO BODY ON IT." They didn't get out of the car. They didn't give me a field sobriety test. I would have failed it. I must have looked spooky to them. The fog was rolling in and the yellow lights overhead did their best to poke holes the night. I was in a gray flight-suit, and a red helmet with a bubble shield.

"Oh, get out of there and give me a hand," I taunted. "You can see there is no body on it."

They looked at each other, said something I couldn't hear, and then shouted. "YOU STAY HERE. WE WILL CALL YOU A TOW TRUCK."

The cops drove away. I lowered the wheel, leaned the bike and me against the wall, and took a break. As the traffic whizzed by, some drivers yelled and a few waved. So far so what.

Going anywhere on this motorcycle was always an adventure in getting back. It broke down all the time. The only safe time was when it wouldn't start. It was German, over-complicated, rare, and unreliable. I had a love-hate relationship with it. Loving it straining full tilt passing uphill on the interstate, or leaning into curves and sweeping myself inches off the pavement. Riding it down country roads, feeling the breeze, smelling the trees and the cool of the crops was heaven.

I hated it when the crank went flat and the engine locked up, in the fast lane on the freeway. The rear tire locked and started smoking. The chain was under tremendous strain. Grabbing the clutch lever, pulling it in, and coasting across three lanes of traffic to the nearest exit, without getting creamed by a Peterbilt, is a dying art. It was weeks waiting for expensive parts to come from Germany. It took all my time, and money.

I had one ticket. The license plate fell off. The cop noticed it was missing, after he stopped to give me a warning about not taking the exit I had signaled for. Had I known the plate was missing, I could have split lanes and left him. What's with California cops? They are the enemy of fun.

Navy corpsmen assigned to emergency rooms don't get much time off. When they do, they try to enjoy it. Sometimes a six-pack of Olympia Beer, some potato chips and some privacy can be like a vacation. I found a large public park and drove to the back of it. I crossed lawns to some shade against a large earthen embankment. I drank the beer, ate the chips, and took a nap.

The police who had their car parked on the lawn telling me, "No motorcycle parking here," awakened me, some hours later. They requested I ride over to the street where they would issue a parking ticket.

Putting on my helmet I noticed the horseshoe logo on a can of beer. It said Good Luck. This was all the encouragement I needed. There were cars passing on the street over my head. It was perhaps 40 feet up through some trees and the slope was over 60 degrees. There was 20 feet of running room. Circling the police car provided 20 more.

I opened the petcock and turned on the gas, tickled the carb, brought the piston to top-dead-center, turned on the key, and stomped on the kickstarter. The engine roared to life and settled down to a fast idle. It warmed while I was cinching the helmet's strap, and pulling on gloves. Every move was slow and deliberate, like Steve McQueen would do it. When all was secure, I pushed the gearshift lever down and clicked it into first gear. Max slowly circled the police car. Passing the trunk, and in their blind spot, rather than leaning right and crossing the lawn to the sidewalk, I leaned left, pinned the throttle and headed for the hill.

Max was in low gear and wide open hitting the foot of that slope. Momentum made the transition from level to upright. The front tire pushed aside anything loose and pressed down the ground cover. The back tire found traction on what was left. I hung on, steered around the trees, and climbed like Jose the hill-climber. If there were shots fired I didn't hear them. All I heard was the engine screaming, the muffler roaring, and the earth moving. I fishtailed and let off the grip, struggled it straight, and pressed on regardless.

Max was out of steam and speed, cresting the rise. Snapping off the gas and coasting down the sidewalk, I waited for a break in traffic. Then, dropped over the curb and fell in among the automobiles. I was lost in suburbia and the cops have radios. I followed the longest line of cars to the freeway. There wasn't another cop, all the way home. It was a close call, but what a rush. This is reason to ride motorcycles. The reward for putting up with the rain, heat, cold, and wind. To go places where cars can't. I also like the headroom, and being able to stand and stretch at stop signs. The problem is the air-conditioning quits at stoplights.

A large tow-truck stopped next to me. It had a crane on the back with a hoist, lots of levers and extra wheels. The driver looked down, and said, "The way we do this is, you hang onto the mirror here, and I tow you off the bridge."

I rolled the bike into position and grabbed one of the horizontal bars of the lower mirror bracket. I put my left foot on the peg, and since the right peg had been chewed off by a passing Mustang, I put my right foot on the rear brake pedal. Big mistake. He drove away. I followed. The bike stayed put. I was dragged off. When my nuts raked the tank, it took the fight out of me. As my toes closed on the handlebars I started yelling, "WAIT, HOLD IT, STOP, STOP!" He stopped. The bike fell over. The headlight broke, and the juice ran out the battery. I fell down.

I was worried about the oil. There is always a puddle of it where you stop to pay your toll. It leaks from cars, trucks, buses and both ends of what ever is parked over it. After paying the toll, be careful how you roll. Both tires have been through it, and they are slick. You can expect the front to slide and the rear to spin. I had made it up to speed and was passing, in the far left lane, when the motor quit. The coil went south. No spark, no power, grab the clutch, coast to a stop, hop off and push, and look professional. Oil wasn't the problem after all.

While pushing Max, the sports car hit it. The Ford had spinner hubcaps that chewed the right peg off and sent it flying down the bridge. I never saw it again.

What I did see was a sign that read, "Treasure Island Exit One Mile". Then others that read, "No Standing, Walking, Hitchhiking, Foot Traffic, Fishing or Bicycles on Bridge."

Cars kept coming closer. I was afraid the next one might hit the bike and take me with it. I pushed along rationalizing the aspects of getting caught with and without the motorcycle. The night was chilly. If you're chilled riding a motorcycle, get off and push. You warm right up. The concepts were too abstract for me, and being a man of action, decided to toss the bike over the bridge and walk the mile, to the base, without the bike. It was a good idea, but poor timing.

The tow-truck guy waited while I picked up the bike, and pushed it into position. This time I put my right foot on the engine case, which was cool by now. With my right hand on the mirror I nodded okay, and off we went, again. We were in the fast lane and he wasn't about to hold up traffic. We were passing cars in the slower lanes. At 70 miles an hour I looked down and saw the curb sawing inches from the wheels. My exit signs were flashing by and I thought: what am I going to do? He is going to want at least $30.00 for this tow and I have three dollars on me. As the curb dissolved into my exit on the left, I let go, laid it low, and he shot on to San Francisco.

A shower of sparks, like welder's popcorn, cut the dark behind me, as the frame scraped the black top. I held both brakes and scrubbed off speed. The road curved left and downhill. With no lights I judged where the road ended, stepped off the bike, kept it rolling fast, and shoved it over the edge. It went crashing downhill to the ocean. I rubbed by hands and said to no one in particular, "That is a load off my mind."

"There is no parking down there." I turned and saw a sailor, standing there in all white. He wore white leggings, a wide, white, web-belt dangling a nightstick, and a .45-caliber pistol. He wore a chrome helmet. A navy blue band on his left sleeve, with a yellow SP on it, covered his rate. I couldn't tell if he was a boot-recruit or a Chief Warrant Officer. It didn't matter. I know the look. Shore Patrol rhymes with bad news.

I asked, "Can I get it tomorrow, in the daylight?"

"No. You will get it now. This is a military reservation and there is no parking down there." Behind him was a little guard shack with a bare light bulb and a telephone.

If you are in the military, and you mess with the civilian police, the military will protect you, up to a point. If you are in the military and you mess with the military police they have several things they can do to you, none of which are pleasant. Except for that one time in Juarez, Mexico, when they chased us from bar to bar, after curfew, I don't mess with the military police.

I said, "Here, I'll get it," and took one step over the edge and fell into the night. I careened off trees, stumbled and tumbled through the Chico brush, tripped on the deadfall, and kept going. I did a half gainer on a low-lying limb; cart wheeled down hill and added new dimensions to the term bushwhacked. I stopped when my head hit a tree, and I went to sleep.

I awoke to voices. One said, "Sure has been a lot of fun getting down here," rather facetiously.

Another said, "I can't remember having a worse time," more sarcastically.

The third admonished me with, "You wouldn't have these problems, if you would just stop screwing up." There was no one else around. I always wake up like this.

My breath had stopped fogging the face-shield because the helmet was full of leaves. I removed it and dumped the contents. Using a handkerchief, kept for this purpose, I wiped off the mud and rocks adhered to the bubble.

I cannot over-emphasize the importance of safety gear. Heavy boots, heavy gloves, leather jacket and pants, helmet and earplugs are a hassle. They don't help you home hanging in the closet when you need them. Even if you are just riding down to check the mail, always put it on. It can save you weeks of healing. I haven't dropped a bike in a decade, but I always dress for a fall.

It was darker than inside a cow and the only point of reference was a glow from the guard shack bulb. It looked to be directly overhead and about halfway to the moon. Rolling on my stomach, I began inching towards it. Then, I was lucky. I found the motorcycle on the way up. While groping for a handhold, I touched the rear tire. Max was laid on its side and wedged in pretty good. I managed to climb on top of it. Then I heard voices. The tow-truck was back.

"Did you see some nut come by here on a motorcycle?" The driver shouted at the guard.

"No one on a motorcycle has come by here, sir," he honored the driver. Technically this was true, since I left the road some yards before his shack. The military protects it own.

"Well, he's got to be around here somewhere," threatened the driver.

"You better keep looking," was the reply. The tow-truck left.

The bike wasn't that far down. It only took two hours of struggling, tugging, lifting, pulling, pushing, prying, and straining to gain the shoulder. You talk about an aerobic workout and total body training; I was soaked in sweat and seeing stars. This was quite possibly the second hardest thing I have ever had to do. I rolled it past the shack and leaned it against the outside of the guardrail.

Sitting on the rail to plot my next move, I felt a hand touch my shoulder. "Hey buddy, you look like you've had a rough night." It was a black man in the chrome helmet. There must have been a shift change.

I said, "Don't get me started."

He said, "Why don't you go get some rest?"

I sighed, "I will. I just need to do something with this bike."

"Leave it there," he insisted. "It'll be okay."

I felt better, stood up, shook his hand and said, "You are every bit of all right."

It was a long walk up hill to the base, but it was a piece of cake. I showed my ID to the sentry. The jarhead said, "I've never had anyone walk on board."

I was tired and searching for something witty to say, intoned, "You are young yet." He let me pass and I walked the row of 40 barracks that all looked the same. I found the one where

I stayed, went in and took a hot shower. I shaved, put on a clean uniform and fell in for morning muster. It was dawn.

They called my name. I walked to the podium and a Chief Petty Officer handed me my orders. Glancing at them, walking back to my number on the grinder, I read, "Assigned to the Fleet Marine Force, Third Marine Division, Republic of Viet Nam." My departure date was the next day.

After falling out and going in to change clothes, I found a note on my bunk. It was from security, and read, "We have your motorcycle." Some things in life you can delay. Some things require immediate attention. This was something that couldn't wait. If security has to look for you, their attitude is different when dealing with you. I walked back to the front gate, deciding to play it dumb and see what happened. Volunteer no information.

It was a small room with a few Marines behind a counter. I showed one of them the note. He said, "We brought your bike up and it is in the impound lot."

"Can I leave it there?"

"No. You have until noon to remove it."

"Does anyone here want to buy a motorcycle?" There were no takers.

While the others went to breakfast, I went to the phone. I called a brother of mine living in Sacramento. He was in the Air Force and lived off base. He said he would take the bike; or rather I could leave it there. I called a place that rented pickup trucks, but you had to be over 25 years old. I wasn't. I asked around and found someone who was, and who, for a fee, would drive the truck-after I paid for the rental and bought the insurance.

Mr. Up and Up had a car and a friend named Larry. It was a package deal. The car was a bonus. I didn't have to pay a taxi to take us across town. Larry was one of the biggest men I have ever met. He was from Kentucky and covered with hair. We came back to the impound lot with the truck. One of the Marines snarled, "Why don't you wash that thing?" He was referring to the mud and dirt encrusted on the bike.

"I tried, twice, last night," but I didn't elaborate.

Larry loaded the bike by himself. He started it rolling and levitated it into the back. Holding it upright he asked, "Do you have any tie-down straps?"

"Let it flop," I growled. He laid it down gently. Then he climbed into the cab and took up two-thirds of the seat. Mr. Up and Up sat behind the wheel. I climbed in the bed, kicked the scoot in disgust and stretched out. We went to Sacramento.

Through a series of hand signals and shouts from the cab and back we found my brother's house. He was waiting. Larry unloaded the bike by himself. He rolled it across the lawn and leaned it against the only tree. My brother insisted on chaining it to the tree.

I said, "No one is going to steal that thing. You would be lucky if they did. I left it in downtown San Francisco for two days, with the key in it, and nobody took it." He was worried and chained it anyway.

He had to go to work. As we walked to the truck, I mentioned my orders and the fact I was going to war tomorrow.

"Have you told Mom and Dad?"

I related I hadn't, but promised to write them as soon as I had a new address. We were born eleven months apart. He is older I am bigger. So we are more like twins. He shook my hand. There were tears in his eyes.

The ride back was uneventful. I lay in the bed of that truck and felt like Lindbergh after crossing the Atlantic and looking for Paris. Awake for 33 hours, hungry, hung-over, exhausted and everything hurt. We returned the truck early and had money coming back. We blew it on steaks and beers at the enlisted men's club and went to bed.

The next morning a bus took us to the airport. We boarded a World Airways jet and flew 18 hours to Da Nang. A truck hauled some of us north to Quang Tri. I walked in a tent to be assigned, and found someone I knew. The tent held a file cabinet and a desk. Behind the desk was Dave. We went to school together at Balboa Naval Hospital in San Diego, and later worked as staff at Oak Knoll. His father was an Admiral on active duty in the Navy. No wonder Dave was in the rear with the gear.

He stood, smiled, came from behind the desk, shook my hand and said, "I saw you were coming," referring to his clipboard. "I never got the chance to thank you for grossing out my mother. Do you remember that party we had at my place?"

I remembered it. It was a bunch of high-school kids dancing to records in the basement. They had blacklights and posters. Everybody was paired and I was the odd man out. They weren't drinking beer, smoking cigarettes, or doing drugs. Not really my crowd. I had a buzz going in and when it left, so did I. "Yeah...sure." I hesitated.

He reminisced, "My mother and I were standing in the front room looking out the window. Your motorcycle was parked on the lawn. It was leaking fluids and she was worried about it killing the grass. You walked up. Started kicking it and it wouldn't start. It fell over and you started yelling at it. Then you jumped up and down on it and kicked it. Then you unzipped your pants and pissed on it. I never laughed so hard in my life. It was even funnier because my mother was so appalled. Then you picked it up, got back on it, coasted down the driveway, popped the clutch, and drove away."

He was laughing again. I hoped he had a sense of humor. He said, "I have been saving this job for you." And, with a stroke of luck, he assigned me to Headquarters Company Ninth Marines. I became the personal corpsman of Colonel Robert H. Barrow, who later became General and Commandant of the Marine Corps.

It was no cakewalk, but it could have been worse. Thanks to him, I visited parts of Laos, Cambodia and North Viet Nam. People ask if I still fly in helicopters. I tell them, "No, it just isn't the same without ground fire coming through the floor."

Colonel Barrow is one of the greatest Marines of the 20th century. I angered him once, by getting a speeding ticket in an ambulance during a rocket attack. He put me to work at Graves Registration for three days. Don't anger the General. He provided that lovely morning our position was over run by the North Vietnamese Army, and it was hand-to-hand-combat.

I came back without a scratch. A C-141 returned me a year later. My brother picked me up at Travis Air Force Base. Late into a bottle of Tequila I asked, "Whatever happened to Max the motorcycle?"

"Oh, I put some parts on it and got it running. I was riding it around. One day up by Lodi it quit on me, as I was crossing a bridge."

"Was it a river bridge?"

"No, it was more like an irrigation canal. The water was deep. There was no guardrail. I rolled it in and it sank. I figured you wouldn't mind."

I smiled. With any luck, someday, it will wash into the bay. So I can always say, "I know where it is."

BOBBY

During the Tet Offensive in 1968, Bobby made the whiskey run. He took the ambulance to the airstrip, and hitched a helicopter ride to Quang Tri. He walked to a place where he could buy a case of gin for 80 cents a bottle. He would hop on a helicopter flying to Khe Sanh. When it landed, he was on his own agenda. He would run from fox-hole to fox-hole selling the bottles for $20 each. I was right behind him with my case of gin. We would rather see them sucking gin than shooting heroin.

We grabbed the money and ran up the back ramp of a CH47 just lifting off. There were two bags of mail we tossed on top of seven dead Marines. We sat on the bags and watched the two forward gunners lay down a line of lead. The rotor blades were popping, grabbing hot air lifting out of there. Bullets whizzed through the cabin. They came through the bulkheads and up from the deck. Hot hydraulic fluid sprayed from holed lines. Fuel leaked from somewhere above. The motors whined. The fuselage filled with smoke and shell casing, from the two machine guns. We felt bullets pummeling the bodies beneath us as we gained altitude.

All the Plexiglas was shot out of the portholes, so the smoke cleared as soon as we were out of range. One of the gunners looked our way and noticed us for the first time. We were the only passengers. Bobby and I gave him a thumbs up. He saw the black Caduceus on our helmets, and recognized us as being in the Hospital Corps. He said something into his mouthpiece that we couldn't hear, and we flew on to Quang Tri. We helped unload the dead at Graves Registration, like we had a purpose, caught a flight back to the base and drove the ambulance back to the hooch.

I only went on the one run. It was a fine way to filet a flak jacket, but a hell of a way to make 230 bucks.

Whatever else you do in life, learn to type. The ability to type kept me off the op. The op was any operation that Colonel Barrow had planned. A report was due once a month, perfectly typed, describing all that had been done by the medical staff.

Bobby couldn't type, so he would go on the op. He was out snooping and pooping in the bush while I was in the hooch with the typewriter. The report could have been typed in a day. I took a week.

When I arrived at Vandegrift Combat Base (VCB), Bobby was the First Class Petty Officer. There was also a Doctor, a Chief and a Third Class Petty Officer. The third wanted to be Davy Crockett and transferred out. He wasn't replaced.

Bobby was a gambler, blue-eyes, smiling, beer-belly, and balding. He was the first man to welcome me aboard, and show me the ropes. Bobby played poker. He took everybody's money. We were paid once a month, in military script. The first week after payday the hooch tabled the game. I put my money in military savings and earned 10% interest. I didn't think I would ever see it; I just didn't want Bobby to get it.

The other three weeks, after everybody was out of money, we played cutthroat Monopoly. That's where the one-dollar bills become thousands. You can buy property on the first roll, and cover it with hotels. Bobby computed the rent, in his head. He always bought Park Place and Boardwalk and with 10 hotels on each the rent was 15 to 20k. When he wiped you out you gave him all your money and property and vacated the board.

Since Bobby had all the money in camp, he was the one who made the loans. He had an analytical mind and would compute interest daily, monthly and quarterly until he had those kids so confused they took the money and agreed to anything. Suckers would borrow their money back and lose it again in a few games of poker trying to break his winning streak. It never happened. On payday many Marines signed their checks over to Bobby. If you didn't pay Bobby back, by the time you had orders out he would lose your health record.

If you lost your health record, you also lost your International Certificate of Vaccination. At your next duty station you had to take all your shots. There were smallpox, yellow fever, cholera, typhus, typhoid, plague, poliomyelitis, tetanus, and blood typing. Marines hate shots. They take a lot of time and make you sore and sick.

The Marines had a beer ration. A truck would drop pallets of Schlitz, Hamm's and Carling Black Label off in the mud.

Vandegrift was a new base; not a lot of services. The Gunny would issue the beer - a six-pack here, and a case to that tent, until it went. It was consumed warm and we were glad to have it. Bobby saw a way to make a buck in the beer business. He convinced somebody to let him build a place, and get some coolers to chill the beer.

A bulldozer knocked the top off the hill behind our hooch. Bobby paid him off in cold beer. We kept ours in the refrigerator we had to have for the vaccines, serums, and antivenin. We were connected to a generator that ran day and night just out of earshot. The dozer made quick work of the lot and left.

Then Bobby hired some Montagnard people to lay a concrete slab. They hand poured an L-shaped deck some 40 feet by 25 feet long, and 20 feet wide. He found another bunch to erect bamboo poles to hold long cross members to which were attached lattice panels. These were thatched with the local grasses. The walls could be lifted up on nice evenings and closed during the heavy rains. It had a thatched roof, supported by bamboo rafters.

We walked around in it, while the engineers strung some wire and put in outlets at his request. He had an idea for a bar, but couldn't nail two boards together. I had grown up on a ranch in Colorado; where we made everything we needed, usually out of something else. My high school shop teacher was a master carpenter, just like Norm Abram. He knew more tricks than a-half-dozen monkeys on a hundred yards of grapevine. He taught me some of them.

I have an affinity for 3/4" plywood and 2x4 lumber. Bobby provided an abundance of materials and tools. I made a bar. We tested it by having six men stand on it. It was L-shaped and took up the inner corner of the slab. The bar accommodated six high-back chairs and had a foot rail made of bamboo. There were shelves inside, underneath, and money drawers built in. The two beer coolers occupied the space behind us. This was before the days of pop-tops. There was a device with a lever that punched open the cans.

We named it "The Montagnard Bar," after the people who built it. It was billed as "The last stop before the DMZ." It opened at six p.m. and closed at ten p.m. Beers were a buck, a greenback, script, four quarters, or foreign currency, whatever you had. A buck's a buck. The money was pushed through slots in the bar into a locked drawer. We made change from our wallets.

I typed the requisitions. Bobby forged the signatures. We brought all the stuff from Quang Tri in a truck Bobby borrowed from the motor pool. Special Services provided the tables and chairs. Ours was an enlisted men's club. The officers made their own club and had an ice machine and mixed drinks. It was crazy. We worked our asses off opening beers, twisting, turning and lifting. We were paid in funny money and it all went into the box. Bobby kept the books. It was just the two of us working seven nights a week. When Bobby went on the op I did it by myself.

For entertainment we had a reel-to-reel tape recorder that blasted the latest rock-and-roll from the states, via some guy's girlfriend. Later on, Bobby scored some telephone poles and some more labor. He made an outdoor movie screen by nailing sheets of plywood to the poles and painting them white. He had benches made from some of the poles and brought back a movie projector. We showed movies. God how the money rolled in.

The bar overlooked the landing zone, almost a mile away. We would watch air traffic on the left, movies in the middle and red tracer streaks of bullets from gun ships shooting up the canyons on the right. Now that's entertainment.

We were building up for an offensive and had been staging ordnance on and around the landing zone. Our troops had also captured much of the enemy's guns and ammunition and it was being stored. One afternoon a Huey sat its tail rotor on a case of something and the whole place started blowing up.

It took three days and nights for all the bombs, bullets, mines, howitzer shells, mortar shells, rockets, TNT and dynamite to expend itself. There were bunkers around the strip and those lucky enough to make it to one, spent three days getting shell-shocked. It was awesome. After dark, we turned the lights off in the bar to enjoy the spectacle. Periodically a B-52 would drop its bombs on the horizon and arc light the background. Now that's really entertainment.

We had a mixed crowd. There were the regulars from Headquarters' Company, the snipers, motor pool guys and the armorer. Depending on which company was back from the bush, we would have them tell the most horrible stories. The ones from

Charlie one-nine were the most gruesome. Our rear was everybody else's front. Australians, Koreans, French film crews and whoever was passing through visited us.

We had six Army Special Forces troops fresh from the Z one evening. They still had Thermite grenades on their packs, to destroy if captured. They looked like they had been awake and taking speed for five days. They drank beer after beer, didn't talk and didn't blink. They all sat at one table and watched each other's back. We had Green Berets, Recon, Special Forces, Seals, CIA types, Airborne Rangers and Marines raising hell with each other.

There was usually a game of liar's poker being played at the bar. Whoever was holding when the hand was called, had to buy a round for the bar. The Colonel would bring in a General from time to time. We would stagger to attention, and after being told, "As you were," would gather around and drink beer with them and listen to their stories. We were honored by their presence.

One morning the Doctor returned from a staff meeting with a map drawn on a sheet of paper. He told us we had been selected to assist with a United Nations humanitarian effort in the village of Mai Loc. Some Montagnards had been resettled there in the old French town in the foothills of Cam Lo. The plan was to drive our open jeep loaded with medical supplies to the village, see as many people as we could, and be back by dark.

This was fine with us. We liked the Montagnards. They worked for us. They had been driven out of North Vietnam, where all their silver was buried, and were having a tough time. They worked for the highest bidder. Sometimes it was us, sometimes the enemy. Everybody has to eat.

We loaded the Jeep and headed out. I drove. Bobby took shotgun, literally. He had a double-barrel 12-gauge resting on his leg. The Doctor was in the back with the supplies and all the weapons on lock and load. It was a maze of rugged dirt roads, jungles, open fields and streams to cross. While fording one river we were attacked by a water buffalo.

The water was less than two feet deep. We were in the middle of the river when the caribou charged us from up stream. He had horns galore and rammed the spare tire on the back and pushed us. I stepped on the gas to lend some horsepower. The

Doctor jumped up, braced his feet, pointed an M-16 at the animal's head and thumbed off the safety.

Bobby started yelling. "Don't do it Rude. Don't shoot it!" He held his fire. We had heard the story about the Marine who shot one of these animals and had to pay a $10,000 fine to the family. If you owned one of these you had great wealth. It was your transportation, your truck, your tractor, and a source of food, fuel, clothing, and future. You could breed it. As soon as we were pushed clear of the river the animal stretched its neck and bellowed at us, then ambled back upstream.

After three hours of driving we found the village. The people were waiting in a long concrete structure that had seen better days. It was bombed out and had vines growing through it. There was an open trailer full of medical supplies and another with a tank of fresh water. There were a couple of CIA types with sunglasses and radios, running the show. The line was endless. All the kids had scabies. There were many bacterial infections, traumatic amputations, one thing after the other, with the very young and the very old.

The doctor took the worst cases; Bobby and I treated the rest. We took a few minutes for a cold C-ration lunch and kept at it. At about 3:30 p.m. when we had planned to quit and head back, a helicopter landed with more patients. The Doctor talked to the pilot who said not to worry about driving back, we could take the chopper. This was a relief so we kept working. At sunset the Doctor diagnosed an infant with bubonic plague. The child had the classic symptoms including swollen bulbous glands in the groin. As soon as word of the kid's condition was out, the crowd thinned.

He had to be air-evacuated to the Children's Hospital in Dong Ha. We couldn't just send the kid to the hospital. The whole family had to go. The mother, father, siblings, chicken and goat were loaded onto the helicopter. The CIA guys boarded and it lifted off in the failing light. There went our ride.

I heard engines and clanking noises. Several tanks drove into the area. One stopped next to me and a hatch opened. An antenna followed by a human rose out of it. His goggles made him look like a giant bug. He said they were camping there for the night, and his commanding officer was Jimmy Stewart's son. I found him and introduced myself. We talked briefly and I told him how much I enjoyed his father's work as an actor.

I walked back to the jeep and Bobby was filling the gas tank from the jerrican. I asked, "What's up?"

"We're getting out of here," he said.

"Are you crazy?" I laughed. "You want to drive across Viet Nam after dark? Haven't you been listening to the lectures they give us? About how the enemy moves at night, or how they use the dark to their advantage to mine the roads and set booby traps?"

"We have to go check on our bar. I don't trust these Marines."

"Our bar will be fine. I would rather stay here with all this firepower. It's safer than out there alone with rifles."

"It's our business. We have to run it."

I left and found the Doctor. He was examining an old man. I told him, "Hey Rude, Bobby has a wild hare up his ass that we have to go back and check on the bar. Since he outranks me, and I can't tell him no, would you do the honors?"

"Hell no, I'm coming with you."

"What?"

"If I can spent the night in my own bed in my own hooch, I'd rather."

"I want you to know that you are both certifiably insane." He straightened and looked at me sternly, and I said, "With all due respect, sir."

"That's better. Now load up."

We left. Bobby drove. Rude took shotgun. I was in the back with all the weapons. There were rounds in the chambers and the safeties were off. Bobby didn't turn the lights on. He navigated by the faint light of the moon and found our way out. He had remembered landmarks on the way in.

We had the incident with the water buffalo early in the day. Tonight the terror was tigers. Bengal tigers, ten feet long from the nose to the tip of the tail, eight hundred pounds of man-eating mean and moving swift, silent and deadly. The war was in their natural habitat and put a damper on their diet. The animals normally preyed on by the big cats were depleted by the bombings and engagements. The groups of insurgents living off the land were also eating them. The tigers ate anything left, for survival. They would drag bodies away from ambush sights. They ate pilots in downed aircraft.

One came into the compound at Vandegrift. It mauled a man and ran. The next night we were all in foxholes on the perimeter waiting for it. Two men to a hole, back-to-back, eyes on the line scanning 180 degrees. No talking, just listening for anything moving. After a tense hour, word came down the line. A tiger had run from the shadows and grabbed a Marine in a foxhole. The beast crushed the man's larynx before he could make a sound. He broke his neck, suffocated him and dragged his lifeless body away before the other Marine could point and shoot his loaded weapon. The hand is quicker than the eye. The tiger is quicker than the hand.

I was tail-gunner Joe covering our flank for three hours of nerve-wracking, paranoid travel. I expected the Jeep to hit a mine any minute, or a sniper's bullet to get one of us. We saw no people, and no animals. We surprised the sentry at Vandegrift. He didn't expect anyone to be coming down the road. He was there to keep vehicles from leaving. He started giving us gas; until he recognized Rude, then let us pass.

We dropped the Doctor off at the hooch and went to check on the bar. It was closed just like we left it. The chairs were stacked on the tables. It was clean. The tape player was still there and the projector was there.

I started bitching at Bobby. "You see. What did I tell you? Everything is okay. You scared the hell out me for nothing." We walked behind the bar with our flashlights to check on the coolers and found a surprise. There were new padlocks on all the doors. Our locks had been cut and were on the floor. We found new locks on the cash drawers. We walked to the metal shed, where we kept our back-up beer, and found a new padlock there. I apologized. "I am sorry, Bobby. You were right. Something is going on."

Bobby was ready to start raising hell with people. He wanted to get to the bottom of this right now and find out who was responsible. I begged off saying it was late, I was tired and wanted to go to sleep. I reeked of adrenaline and it had been a terrifying day. I crashed.

The next morning Bobby went to see the Top Sergeant and the Gunny. He came back with news. The village of Mai Loc had been attacked and everyone was dead. The world was in a state of shock over the death of Jimmy Stewart's son. The attack had begun just as we were leaving. The enemy force moved in, took the tank crews by surprise, killed them instantly and set fire to their machines. The civilians were dealt with during the long night.

The sergeants told Bobby the bar belonged to the Marine Corps, and they would run it. They thanked us for our help in getting it started, but they would take it from here. Bobby was fuming. He was at his best planning revenge, but before he could do anything, about the bar, the Colonel decided he was going to get the Vietnamese who overran Mai Loc and headed back into the bush. Bobby and Rude went on the op. I helped the Chief with sick call and typed the report.

Two weeks later Bobby returned madder than a wet hen. He had it all planned out how he was going to get the bar back. Who he had to threaten, pay off, wake-up, let in on, cajole, bribe and coerce. I said, "You are on your own. If the Marines want that bar, they can have it."

He was shocked, "What?"

"That place is dangerous. Have you noticed most of the customers are armed? It's not just drunks with automatic weapons; they're sharpshooters and marksmen with attitudes. Now you are great the way you can wade into a standoff and get them to lower their weapons, but even that is risky. They can still punch you in the face and break your nose, teeth, eye or jaw. All it's going to take is for one guy to spray that place with bullets, and at the very least they will close it down. Every time there is trouble, and I hear rifle bolts slamming home, I wish I had put some sheet steel in the bar. I wonder if those beer coolers are bullet-proof, because I feel like jumping behind them."

"It's the money though."

"It's funny money, and it's not worth it to me," I countered.

"Well, I am still going to get it back," he boasted.

I explained to Bobby that while he was gone I had been listening to the scuttlebutt in camp, getting most of my information by taking cold beers to the barber. "The Marines have no problem with me, it's you they were trying to get rid of. You have made some real enemies by taking their money, charging them exorbitant interest on loans and gambling debts. And if they leave, without paying, loosing their medical records."

"What can they do about that? I'm a Corpsman, nobody's going to hurt me."

"Maybe nobody here. These guys can write letters, make phone calls and have meetings." I related that some of the snipers were sending resumes to the mob. They wanted to be hit men after being separated from the service. If some of the guys he crossed were already working for the mob, they would have connections. It could be as simple as someone doing a favor. "The newspapers say the CIA has a working relationship with the mob."

"Yeah, yeah, what's that got to do with me getting the bar back?"

"The reason you lost the bar was they didn't expect you to come back."

"What do you mean by that?"

"I think these guys have put a contract out on you, and the CIA is helping them. And, I think, the whole Mai Loc incident was choreographed for your demise."

"Now you're really out there," Bobby jested.

"Too many coincidences for me."

"For instance?"

"For instance the trailer full of medical supplies. We were led to believe there were a handful of people, and we carried what we supposed we needed. There were so many people. It was like those CIA types knew they were all going to die and felt guilty about it. Instead of a last meal they gave them a last check-up. Why were all the patients flown in? And we had to drive? We worked faster than they thought we would, and when we were almost done, they flew in another load. They gave us false hope saying they would fly us out, and made us stay and work. If it was an international deal why were we the only three medical personnel there? They planted that boy with the plague. I saw a member of the flight crew carry him off the 'copter and hand him to some people in line. But what seals it for me was there was just enough seats on the helicopter for the CIA types and the Vietnamese family. They couldn't even squeeze on Rude to assist the infant."

"But what about all those tanks rolling in?"

"That was just icing on the cake to make us wait, and enjoy the party. Somebody knew that village was going to be hit, and as long as you were there, that's all that mattered. I have your greed and the Doctor's need to thank for saving my life. Your life is still in jeopardy." Bobby didn't argue. He was ashen. "You have a few months left. If I were you I would transfer out of here and change my habits. Don't play poker, don't play games, and don't make loans. Lay low until you rotate home."

Bobby transferred. They didn't replace him. The chief took care of the medical records. I typed the report, and went on the ops.

Several years later I met Jimmy Stewart and his wife at the bar in Hawaii. I didn't tell him I had met his son, and was one of the last people to see him alive. It didn't seem appropriate.

IN HEAVEN

"Hi, my name is In Heaven. You can call me In." He held my hand as I stumbled out of the van. Two men having an argument on a low rock wall I was more or less parked against awakened me. One was a drunk Portuguese Caterpillar Driver and the other was a Jesus Striker, in a blanket. I came around, being an arbitrator in their argument, until I made a move for the john.

"Hey! Where are you going?" questioned the drunk.

"I got to take a piss." I remembered why I was up. "Whoa too much beer..."

"You're supposed to be the arbitrator here."

"I will help you brother." In Heaven took my hand, again, and walked me to the men's room across the park. He confided in a whisper in my ear, "I was tired of arguing with that drunk anyway." It was midnight and he disappeared, just melted into the shadows.

I woke up and told my girlfriend, "I had the weirdest dream."

"I told you not do drink beer and eat those mushrooms. How many times will it take? You either do one or the other."

"That must be it."

"A girl told me there were some mango trees down that road. Why don't you go pick some for breakfast? I will make pancakes."

I grew up where there were no trees. When I was six they took me to town to see the tree. I could always see the tree after that. It was a bush on the horizon. So all trees look alike to me. I walked down the road until I saw the Jesus Striker sleeping in a hammock. He was off the road, back in the jungle. He had hair down to his waist and beard to match. He wore white underpants and his hammock was his blanket tied off with short lines. He had unblemished skin, very tan, no scars, no identifiable marks, no tattoos, and no piercings. He wore no jewelry, rings, necklace or watch. He was not fat, nor was he skinny. He was not muscular but he had tone. He had perfect white teeth and a comforting smile, which he used when I woke him up.

"Mangoes man, you seen any?"

"You passed them. They are back by the park. I will help you pick some." He untied his blanket, wrapped it around him, plucked his toothbrush from a branch and we were off. This was all he owned. He had no money, no bills, no ills, no phone, no shoes, and no home. He was In Heaven. He had no address and no identity.

The trees were easy to find with all the fruit on the ground. We picked a few. In Heaven ate his while we walked and talked. He washed his hands on a faucet we passed and helped himself to a drink of water. He met my girlfriend and left spreading joy and light.

"He is a pleasant fellow," she said, watching him sashay away in his designer cape.

"He was in my dream."

He hung out in the park and we visited with him often. I asked him, "Why don't you hang your blanket in the park?"

"You have to have a permit to be in the park, and it is only good for two weeks. The cops will make you leave if you don't have a permit. You have to go to Hilo to get one and stand in line. Too much hassle for In Heaven. If you are never here, you never have to leave."

I was on Haight in '68. I saw the Hippie movement, and the dropouts, but everybody, no matter how far out, still needs to go to the store. Except In Heaven. He had nothing in common with anyone else I have ever met. He looked like Jesus, but he wasn't a Jesus freak. He prayed, but he didn't pull anybody else into it. He fasted. He would go three days without food, get wasted sitting on a sidewalk leaning against a pavilion wall staring out to sea. We took him water and he was so weak he couldn't speak.

In Heaven had charisma, a magnetic personality, and a following. One of the flock carved him a flute out of bamboo. He played a melodious tune all afternoon, and left it on a picnic table. Someone stole it. He summed it up as, "They needed it more than me but the music will always be In Heaven." If we gave him a book he would sit and read it from cover to cover and abandon it. If there were a $20 bill in the dirt, he would walk past it without picking it up.

He took long walks and long swims and ate all his food raw, whether it be from the sea or a tree. He was a wisp with his comings and goings. There were welfare cases living in the park with their tents and TV sets. In Heaven wasn't on welfare. There were hippies hitchhiking all over the island. You never saw In Heaven on the road.

He moved his residence from tree to tree. "Are you worried about getting busted?"

"No...I just like a change. I have mastered the oriental art of being invisible."

"How's that?" I inquired.

"Well," he went on, "You must first believe that invisible people exist. This is easy to prove. Imagine you left your desk, and while you were gone someone put a file on it. When you came back you saw the file, but not the person. That was an invisible person. Then you must dress conservatively. Your clothes must not attract any attention. I get around that one by not having any clothes. Then you must clear your mind of all thoughts. This is the hardest thing to do. Everything vibrates and if your mind is on something, or in turmoil, it vibrates. You send out vibrations. Keep your mind blank and you can walk across a crowded room and no will know you are there."

In Heaven could relax on a rock. We would kick back and I would tell him jokes. He always got the joke because of his intellect. He never condemned a joke, or criticized a joke, or expanded a joke. He was just impressed that anyone would know so many jokes and remember them. He thanked God for sending me to him. When I told him the same joke again he would not stop me. He would listen and say, "I enjoyed it better that time." In Heaven was a trip.

He was keen on how words interact to make a joke and tried to think of all the ways to use his name in a sentence. He would say, "To walk with In, to be with In, to live with In." I kept trying to figure In out and we had this conversation often.

"So did you like have a career and a life with a social security number before?"

"All that stopped when I became In Heaven."

"Is this Heaven?"

"No, this is Spencer Park."

"Is Hawaii Heaven?"
"No, Hawaii is an Island."
"Where is Heaven?"
"Where ever I am In."
"I see. Did you hear the one...?"

We were beachcombers and lived off the land. We foraged for food and hiked into the forest and the valleys where the fruit was just falling off the trees. We brought a load of avocados back to the park. In Heaven was helping me sort them. He was marveling at their size and texture and the wonder of God's work. He picked up a soft one with black spots on it and threw it in the discard pile. He said, "Hell with that one. No room In Heaven for that one." And, he laughed because he had made a joke. It was like a new plateau on his learning curve, to be a world citizen.

Word came down the coconut wireless that a local family was taking over the pavilions for the weekend. There was going to be a wedding and a luau. If you are not invited, don't attend. This will be a real local party. There will be a fight; a divorce and the police will show up. The police had already shown and were checking permits and busting squatters. We needed a place for the weekend and In Heaven recommended a secluded beach over 30 miles down the coast. Since it was his idea he said, "No alcohol, tobacco or drugs."

This limited the crowd to my girlfriend and me and it was a sacrifice. It was all right with her if I wanted to dry out. He told us where it was, which dirt road to take off the main highway and what to look for. "There is a cave we can sleep in."

I said, "Aren't you coming with us? You can just show us the way."

In Heaven looked sad and said, "I don't ride in vehicles, or anything with wheels."

"What do you do ride, a donkey?"
"I don't ride on animals either."
"How do you plan on getting down there?"
"I will meet you there." He sat on the rock wall where I met him and waved as we left.

The coast road from Hapuna beach to The Kona Village Resort was new, and we made good time into Kailua. We shopped for fresh fruits and vegetables, filled our water jugs, iced everything down and backtracked to the turn-around. We took the turnoff until it became so rocky and steep we thought if we did get down there we wouldn't get out. We left the van after filling both backpacks and carried the chest between us. It was hot and rough going and we saw a beach, which we reached, but no cave. We walked over rocks to the next little spot of sand, and then over more rocks to the next little spot of sand. And we walked until we came to fairly large beach. We knew this was the right one because In Heaven was standing on it.

"What did you do? Have Scotty beam you down?"

"Scotty who?" he deadpanned.

Of all the things in life that make me wonder, how In Heaven got to that beach takes the cake.

The cave was a low lava tube with a sand floor. It would sleep three but none of us could stand up. We stowed the stuff and looked around. Black lava fingers ran from the cinder cones upland and dry grass filled the patches of dirt. The sun sat behind us and turned the mountains turquoise and the hills gold.

In Heaven was down on fire so we made a cold camp. We ate a little fruit, lay in the warm sand and watched the stars. In Heaven explained that although it felt like we were laying down looking up, we were actually pinned to the planet and looking down. If we were to let go we would fall down into space. In Heaven was so far out the air was thin.

I woke up refreshed and left the cave. It was a gorgeous day. The sun was rising over the mountains behind us. There were a few clouds off shore. A rainbow extended over the little bay. The waves were rolling in four feet high. In Heaven and five dolphins were body surfing. They all had big smiles on their faces and looked like they had never been happier. The dolphins waited in a circle, and barked at one another, while In Heaven swam back out to join them and surf in again.

The ocean went flat. The dolphins dived for the last time. In Heaven waded ashore. He had a large red fish in his hands. He was peeling back the skin with his teeth and eating the meat. The fish flapped its tail, against In Heaven's cheek, and opened and closed its mouth while bulging its eyes. I didn't know if he had caught the fish or if the dolphins had given it to him.

He walked passed me to the edge of the beach and buried the bones in the sand. He came back, picking his teeth with a Keawe thorn. He sat next to me on the cool sand and said, "God gives every bird his food. He just doesn't put it in the nest."

"How is sashimi in the morning?"

"Damn fine brother, you should have some. Everything out of the ocean you can eat raw. Everything out of fresh water must be cooked. That is why In Heaven is next to the ocean."

"I like mine with soy sauce and wasabi and beer."

"That's what separates us from the lower animals. Our ability to condom size." (He had meant to say, "condiments on the side.") And we both laughed. He had made another joke.

"It's a nice morning," I admitted.

"There is a heavy dew. This is a portent of a fine day."

The girl joined us and asked, "Been swimming? I smell fish."

We lay around and rested until it became hot, and then went swimming. In Heaven placed his blanket off to one side of the beach, in the scrub, and sat on it. He folded his legs, rested his hands on his knees, sat very straight and meditated. After our swim we ate more fruit, played grab-ass American style, running and laughing, and wrote love letters in the sand.

When the sun was overhead and we were swimming again to cool off, In Heaven joined us. He swam past us with his hair tied with a piece of line. He dog-paddled around looking under the water and then he dived. After a minute of holding his breath I thought he has pretty good lungs. After two minutes I thought we wouldn't be seeing him again.

A black fish broke the surface. In Heaven rose up with it clutched in his hand. He exhaled and handed it to the girl. She politely refused. He handed it to me. I said, "No Thanks."

He looked at the fish, and said, "Perhaps you're right" and threw it over his shoulder. He dived again and came up with a handful of purple-black seaweed. He offered me a piece. It tasted fishy. He gave some to the girl. She tasted it. Once was enough for her. He ate the rest and dived again. This time he came up with two sea urchins. He ate them both, threw the shells and spines over his shoulder and swam in. He found a thorn, to pick his teeth, and settled back on his blanket.

She looked at me perplexed. I said, "And you ask me if I know Pancho Villa? Hey, we had lunch together."

Later as we were trying to drown each other by fighting over an air mattress in deep water I glanced at In Heaven. There was a lavender light around him and he was levitated eleven inches off his blanket. I blinked and focused again. The scene had changed, the light was gone and he was back on the ground.

I figured it was a trick of the light. That night, while he slept, I examined his blanket. I used my penlight to check the corners and the material. It appeared to be an ordinary dirty, white blanket you would find at a thrift shop, yard sale or plane wreck. There were no switches or wires to indicate flight controls. It wasn't a magic carpet.

We spent two days living on cold food and relaxing. In Heaven ate none of our food or drank our water. He found a spring out on the lava while looking at carvings left by the ancients. He dove down to where fresh water was seeping into the bay and drank that. He told me, "Coconuts are a source of fresh water on islands."

I never saw him eat a bug, but I wouldn't put it past him. Geronimo ate bugs. Bullets would bounce off his skin. There is something in bugs that is good for the skin.

In Heaven ate a variety of things, including leaves, branches, flowers, roots, berries, and fruit, while walking around with me. "Enzymes are the secret to life. Dead food has no enzymes."

On Monday morning we left him there. He was happy. We had things to do. We finally made it out with the van and up the road to the highway. We tried to put a label on In Heaven, the way you put things into categories and make them easier to deal with. He didn't fit, and was hard to tag.

The girl said, "For all his passive banality he scares the hell out of me. He projects a persona that covers his efforts to shield an inner malevolence. He has an arrogance that is suppressed and a superior attitude that's disturbing. He makes me feel like he always knows more than anybody else."

She reads too many books and always says things like this. Nobody knows what she is talking about. "You don't think he would hurt you, do you?"

"I think there is a side to him he hasn't shown us and we don't want to see. I don't think he would hurt me as long as I am with you. He likes you because you make him laugh."

"So, do you think he is an alien?" I asked.

"No, I don't think he is an alien. He might be a wizard, and if so a very old one, because he can contain his wizardry."

I said, "If you don't want to tell me what you think, that's okay."

"What you should be asking yourself is, do wizards go on vacation?"

"Keep talking. I'm listening."

"If you were a wizard living in a cave, in Scotland, and the fire could barely keep up with cold and wind, wouldn't you think hanging a hammock in Hawaii would be In Heaven? When you go on vacation you leave your friends behind, right? What if fire is your only friend?"

You can buy into that if you want, but I decided he was terminal. He had leukemia, or cancer and was on his way out. He had come to grips with it and the realization was reflected in his inner contentment.

A year later we were at Middle Keei beach cooking breadfruit in our van. I handed a plateful out to a Hippie, in the dark. He handed it back asking, "Have you got any without pepper?"

I said, "Pepper is the first spice."

He said, "Pepper is an intestinal irritant. If you want to live forever, don't eat spices. That's the secret to immortality. If you have already eaten spices it is too late. You might as well keep eating them."

I moaned, "How come nobody tells me these things before it's too late?"

"If everybody found out early, there would be too many people In Heaven."

MR. MEYER

There is a railroad around Disneyland. Small steam engines pull carloads of people past vistas through the park. Recorded messages detail the history and construction of the different areas. Walt Disney loved trains. When things were too much in the office he would put on his overalls, don his striped cap and become the engineer. The customers never knew it was Mr. Disney himself who was at the controls and driving the train. He did it to escape the pressure of the place, and as a diversion to think up a solution to a particular problem.

My boss is the same way. When it gets to be too much to handle upstairs, he will come down to see me. Whatever is on his mind will change. Whatever was bothering him will either be forgotten or be looked at in a different way. We don't talk shop. I either tell him jokes, listen to his troubles, or amuse him with an incident involving the guests. Sometimes he comes by just to make sure we are telling the people the same thing. "Let's get our stories straight."

As the years roll by his drink changed from a rum and coke to a beer, to white wine, to Perrier water. Like a King in disguise he will stare at the ocean, visit with the customers and ignore the employees. That makes him easy to be around. If he is recognized, he will buy drinks for the bar and depart. If the bar is busy, he will remain anonymous and enjoy his drink.

One afternoon he showed up, looking beat. I called him by his real name and he sat down. A couple walked over and asked if he was the General Manger of the hotel. He stood, introduced himself, shook hands and they started in. "The plane was late; the luggage was lost; the room wasn't ready; the help is surly; the food sucks and there are ants in the tub."

He is a professional Innkeeper. He said, "Yes sir and yes ma'am. I will do what I can. I am sorry about that. I will take care of that. Someone will be there to take care of the ants. If there is anything I can do, call me." They left and he walked over and picked up the phone. He dialed his secretary and requested that a bottle of wine, a fruit basket, and card be sent to their room. He walked back over to me and glared, "From now on you call me Mr. Meyer."

The next day he was showing some VIPs around the hotel and stopped at my bar. I said, "Hello, Mr. Meyer, how are you?"

He was shocked by the retort, and, at a loss for words, blurted out, "Fine, George."

He has called me George ever since. No one else calls me George. I am honored by the nickname. Customers, who know me and have heard of him, find it remarkable that I could work for somebody so long who doesn't know my name. He knows my name, and over the years has had several chances to kill me, but he never has. He feels every organization needs a loyal renegade, and he keeps me around.

His greatest asset is his restraint. It would be very easy to change things and put his signature on the resort, but he understands the market. We house the movers and the shakers of the world. For them, everything changes faster than they can keep up. Their careers, marriages, locations, houses, cars and desires are fleeting. We are the one standard in their life. To come back to a place that is comfortable and never changes is priceless. The resort opened in 1965 and Mr. Meyer has done his best to make time stand still. His motto is, "Don't change anything unless it benefits the guest, the employees and the managers. Don't play one against the other and don't change just to keep up with the competition."

He is from a little country that was absorbed by Germany during World War Two. It doesn't exist anymore. He was a 10-year-old boy when bombs were falling all around and there was nothing to eat. After the war his father started a restaurant and worked him hard. He wanted to be a Veterinarian. He loves animals. Once you are in food and beverage it is hard to get out. He trained in Paris, worked in first-class places, and became one of Europe's finest, before moving to Arizona to become a cowboy.

He opened a restaurant in Arizona that failed. He confided in me, "If you want to ruin your life and your marriage, open a restaurant."

He returned to Inn keeping and worked the Virgin Islands, Puerto Rico, Wyoming and then Hawaii. He has been 27 years at the same desk. This is unusual in the hotel business. You change properties every few years or you don't advance. This property is the top of the heap. Where do you go from here? There is no better resort in the world. He stays around and treats everyone like family.

After 20 years his friend Arte Johnson held him a roast. I had two jokes, but was working and missed it. I will use them now.

When I first started at the resort, Mr. Meyer took me aside and said, "It is very important to call these guests by name. That makes them feel welcome and important."

I said, "I am new here. How am I going to know their names?"

He said, "Look at the luggage tags. That's how I can tell who they are." So together we welcomed Mr. and Mrs. Simulated Leather.

One night I was in the gourmet dining room bar and a waitress returned a drink saying a customer didn't like his Mai Tai. I found the guy in the dining room and while explaining the selling points of the drink, poured it on his jacket. I was most apologetic saying, "Let me take that to get it cleaned," and left with it. Mr. Meyer, seeing my predicament, ordered the guy out of the dining room for violating the dress code.

I left a misbehaving motorcycle at the Honda Dealers in Kona. When it was ready, I put on my leathers and went out and sat alongside the road on my crash helmet with a little sign. One side said "KONA" and the other said "MOTHER." While I was hitchhiking Mr. Meyer came riding by on his bicycle. I held up my thumb and flashed him "KONA."

He said, "You must be kidding?"

I flipped the sign and flashed him "MOTHER." He laughed so hard he clenched his fists and locked his brakes. He fell off his bicycle; just like Johnson's tricycle trick on "Laugh In."

Mr. Meyer rides horses and raises dogs. He loves cats and catches them on the grounds and his buddy the Vet fixes them so we don't get overrun with them. He takes pride in the birds in his ecosystem and it pleases him when the five wild turkeys that live on the golf course take a walk through the gardens and down to the pool. He is more than a resort director; he is the steward of a sanctuary.

It has been my luck in life to serve with men and women who are the very best in their field.

He is famous for his: "You can have breakfast with me if you are up at 5:30." He sits a big table in the dining room and any employee, manager, guest, newsperson, or lawyer who wants to pick a bone with him, will find him waiting. He makes himself available and works the crowd. The last time I saw 5:30 a.m. was when I got home late.

I go in at noon and work until dark. As I'm leaving at 8:00 p.m. he will be running down the back hall changing jackets, and heading for another function. The poor guy, the only time he is afforded the luxury of an eight-hour day is when he is on vacation.

He spends as much time in airplanes promoting the hotel at far away destinations as he does on the property. Yet he will always take time to come by the bar and ask me if there is anything I need. He says he envies my position and I have the job he wants. Just to hang out all day on the beach and look at the girls is heaven. He is the kind of man you want to work for.

FRED

Driving across L.A. in his Lexus listening to George Jones, Fred is down home. He is a big, handsome Irish man, who wears blue aloha shirts. He always has something witty to say, and says it slowly as if straining to think it up. It's all in his delivery. He listens to my jokes over and over and always laughs. It is his charm. He is a rascal of the Pacific jetting to Hong Kong to make a deal, and then to Singapore for some more. Fred is a smart man because he knows everything. He is a wise man because he knows everybody. He deals with kings and emperors, tribal chiefs and heavy hitters. He makes big deals, and then cools his heels at the beach bar, just to check the recipe.

Fred invented the Fredrico. He paid for all the research, in more ways than one. How do you put a price on brain cells? People were saying, "I'll have whatever the man on the floor is having." This is the only place where you can get a Fredrico, and it is the best selling drink in the resort. Fred says it's because of the recipe. I tell him it's the marketing. I use Fredrico subliminal messages on Fredrico people. They never Fredrico know what Fredrico hit them. How many would you like? You should have several while you are in the area. The sooner you have a Fredrico, the longer you will have to enjoy them. After three they are so smooth, they will probably become your tropical drink of choice while in the islands. People have dreams about Fredricos before returning to the source. It is real value for your drink dollar. One Fredrico tastes like another.

The origin of the drink is shrouded in mystery like that thing in Turin. It was in the summer of '88 that Fred and Rick were looking for something different. Tired of sweet drinks, Mai Tais, Pina Coladas, Fruit Daiquiris and Chi Chi's, they wanted something fruity, tropical, and not too sweet. The pair came to the bar after golf and took a scientific approach with the research, until sundown. They found Jack Daniel's cut the sweet, and Bacardi rum was needed to make it tropical. The fruit juices were handy and many combinations were tried. The research was prolonged because nothing was written down, or remembered from one day to the next.

A Fredrico is a shot of Jack Daniel's Black, a shot of Bacardi Rum Silver, and a shot of pineapple juice, orange juice, and passion fruit juice, with two shots of guava juice. Use frozen concentrate juices and mix them double strength. If the directions say mix three-to-one with water, mix it one and one-half to one. Blending it with ice makes it normal strength. To use regular strength or fresh juice, on the rocks or blended, will make it taste watered-down. Doubling the guava juice gives it the local color. It is blended with just enough ice to smooth it and float a cherry. Once perfected, a good time was had by several.

The next day Fred was back, ready for another. Rick was pushing a palm tree and watching ants crawl across the sidewalk. He looked at me hollow-eyed and said, "That is Fred's drink." He stepped back from any fame and legendary status and became the Existential Hero.

Fred shouldered the yoke of celebrity and carries it well. The thing about having a drink named after you is when you walk into a bar you buy everybody that drink. Fred never flinches when the bill is presented and sets the standard for the consumption. He takes the garnish and straw and lays them on a napkin and says to anyone near, "Quaff medicine" and then quaffs it, and sets down an empty glass. He will say to someone sipping his or hers, "If you don't drink it in nine seconds, it tends to a marble out like a fine piece of meat."

Then he will turn to me and say, "Speaking of which. Why don't you buy my daughter over there a Fredrico?" Fred has sons. So any woman walking is the daughter he always wanted. As soon as they stop by to thank him they can't get away without a tattoo inspection. They rub all over him and he gets away with murder.

I pray every night, "God, let me be like Fred."

A most beautiful woman told me she was asleep on a chaise lounge and someone was untying the top of her bikini and making strange noises. When she looked up it was just Fred. She said, "Fred is the only guy who can get away with something like that." I am glad somebody can.

I introduced him to my Doctor's wife. He went over and put his arm around her, and said, "No fondling...too late!" and copped a feel. He got a laugh. She even thought it was funny. Fred is so cool. He is my hero.

The recipe is secret because it is the best way to sell the drink. The Rep from Jack Daniel's had one. As soon as she found out it had Bacardi Rum in it she lost interest in promoting it. The same thing happened when the guys from Bacardi tasted it. Competing brands keep it off the air. You tell people what's in it and they don't want it. Nobody in their right mind would mix these two things together. You tell them it is a secret and they are challenged.

A bartender can lose a sale by being too informative. I was working with a guy when a guest asked him, "What kind of drinks do you make?"

He said, "Mai Tais, Strawberry Daiquiris, Chi Chi's, Margaritas..."

"What's in a Mai Tai?" He revealed the ingredients. "What's in a Strawberry Daiquiri?" Again, he gave away the recipe for that. "What's in a Chi Chi?" I couldn't believe this guy was spilling the recipes. "What's in a Margarita?" He told him how he made the drink. The guy said, "I just need to use the phone."

The next customer asked me, "What do you make?"

I said, "Fredricos."

"What's in it?"

"It's a secret."

"I'll take two."

That's how you sell things. You perpetuate a mystique. A Fredrico is more than a drink it is a situation. Someday, someone will find out you were at this bar and ask if you had a Fredrico. You must say, "I don't remember." Fredricos cause short-term memory loss. They are something you can stick with all day. They are genuine nap insurance. They are good for your golf game. They slow down your back swing and speed up your cart. The drink has a following and you can't buy loyalty like this.

The Fredrico Faithful are at the bar at 10:00 a.m. saying:

"When does this bar open?"

"A fellow could die of thirst before getting a drink around here."

"Come on. You can put that stuff away later. You have paying customers now." If Fred is in the area he cherishes them by buying the first round. He is their Napoleon, their Patton. They will follow him anywhere. Fred knows that a true leader of men washes the feet of his followers. Fred is a legend, and tireless in the promotion of his namesake. The P.R. never stops.

There is a protocol in serving the drink. None are genuine without these lines. If you have one Fredrico we say, "No one has ever died from a Fredrico." This is Fred's line. He won't let me put it on a T-shirt, because it is an implied warranty.

If you have two we say, "They are like used cars. They sell themselves." This is true. If you want to sell a used car, put it on the road with a "For Sale" sign on it. It will do the rest. I used to sell used cars. Our favorite line was, "Bring your wife and title, and we'll dicker."

When you have three Fredricos we say, "I had three Fredricos, and went to brush something off my shoulder, and it was the sidewalk." This is attributed to a regular who wasn't taking care of himself. He had coffee and indigestion for breakfast, and then came to see us at noon. He had one Hebrew National hot dog, without bun, three Fredricos, and fell in mid-sentence. He rolled out of his chair and hit the sidewalk like a 200-pound sack of potatoes. He slammed the slab so hard he set off the seismograph at the Volcano's Observatory.

I left the bar, grabbed his feet and put them on his bar stool the classic shock position. Drunken people must be shown the same care as sick people. It is the law. After some blood ran back to his head, he came around. I helped him back onto the stool. He mumbled a few words and rose up to go to the men's room. He took one step and fell again. I ran out and rolled him over. There was an ambulance on the lawn picking up a drowning victim. I asked him, "You want a package deal on a ride to the Emergency Room?" His eyes rolled back in his head as he passed out. I took that as a yes and sent a bus boy over to the paramedics.

They came over and took his vital signs and then hooked up a portable EKG machine, and ran a tape. A doctor walking by accused them of wasting valuable time since neither one of them could read the tape. But it was procedure for a baseline and they pressed on. They loaded him up and rushed off. That episode cost him $500. His Vegas nerve had shut down, signaling a change in life style. Sooner or later we all turn over a new leaf.

If you have four Fredricos we say, "You are a candidate for the curb-feeler cuff links." This is a Dean Martin joke from Guy, the movie magnate. He knows all the stars and the scenes, every joke and routine. He can do ten minutes of stand-up comedy, leave them laughing and get the order first. He always lands on his feet and is one of the nicest guys in Hollywood. He produced the first Fredrico T-shirt and dressed his golf team in them. He is tireless in his promotion of this beverage and is headed for co-inventor status.

As the material ages and the audience gets younger, it loses its laugh. Curb feelers were on cars in the fifties. There was so much sheet metal you couldn't see where the car ended. The curb feelers were long chrome wires on springs that made noise and allowed parallel parking without damaging the white-wall tires.

When you have five Fredricos we say, "After five, some people have lost their mind." This comes from Henry. He drove Vincent home after setting the record. Henry was an extra in the movie "Waterworld." He was the only one they didn't have to paint gray for the shooting. He was so beat up by the sun he looked like ash.

If you have six Fredricos we don't say anything. We don't want to interrupt the conversation you are having with your shadow.

"You said you would drive me home."

"No. I didn't say anything like that."

"You're lying to me."

"Don't you talk to me like that!"

"I'll talk to you any way I want."

Fredricos bring out the schizophrenia in people, however latent. When they leave I say, "I've enjoyed both of you."

There are record holders. When the drink was invented Fred set the standard at three. To double a standard is a record. The record of seven was set a few months after the invention by Armand Weston. He had seven Fredricos plus a couple of beers to cleanse his palate and left saying, "I'll see you tomorrow." We haven't seen him since.

Vincent DeDomenico Jr. doubled this record on May 4, 1994 by having 14. He did it again on May 5th by having 14 more. He is my Hero. Vincent set the standard for all record attempts. You must adhere to the following criteria to remain championship material.

1. Polite to women. You must stand and offer your chair to any woman who approaches the bar. You must not say anything off color to offend the ladies. You must be a gentleman in all things.

2. Gracious to little children. Vincent would balance them on his shoulders and run down the sidewalk, yelling, giving them the ride of their lives, much to the consternation of their parents.

3. Mr. Public Affairs to the men. Wherever they have been, you have been, and are capable of discussing any region on the globe, political incident, or government's intent.

Any deviation from these criteria will void the record attempt. Some newlyweds challenged the record one afternoon and set out to break it. After five drinks her head hit the bar. Her husband pulled her up by her hair and looked her in the eye. There was no one home. He let go of her hair and her head banged twice on the bar. That did it. The judges decided he was no longer championship material and stopped the attempt. Any one can judge. You only have to sit and watch.

The record now stands at 15 Fredricos. The current champion is Tarek Atassi and he accomplished this on September 2, 1996.

All of these men are champions. If you encounter them in your walk of life, they must be afforded all the respect due their achievement.

The institution where I work does not sanction, allow, encourage, endorse, recommend or recognize record attempts. All attempts must begin at noon and end at dark. Last call is sunset. The judges determine dark. We have a license to protect, and drinking contests are illegal. One may not give away food to sell drinks or give away drinks to sell food. Do not broadcast your intent. The only way to prove you have broken the record is to have a check in front of you with the drinks listed and witnesses or judges of your participation. If you break the record, someone will send you a T-shirt.

It is a perfect world when the sun is setting on the Pacific and everybody is drinking Fredricos. As the golden glow of the primary shadow falls on the glasses and I fill the blender again I call, "Now making Fredricos. Who's in?"

"I'm in." Fred is always in. The last time I saw him the wind was whipping his shirt up his back, his wristwatch was blown up to his elbow, he was head into it. There was sand on the foam of his drink. He sets a fine example for little children everywhere.

BILL

This old man he put a hole in me. It was on the deep blue sea on a Hobie 16 catamaran. I was holding a plastic T-handle on a stainless-steel shroud. There was supposed to be a harness, but Bill didn't have it. We had the windward hull up and the rudder was starting to sing when the leeward hull sliced into a wave and it was all stop. Everything stopped but me. I sailed out to the end of the cable and came back between the hulls and stopped when I hit the dolphin striker. It took a chunk of meat right above the wallet pocket on my shorts.

I crawled on the trampoline feeling like there was an arrow in my right kidney, and Bill asked, "Are you Okay?"

I looked up and focused through salt-encrusted sunglasses on him and said, "Yeah, I guess."

"Well sit up, pussy! You are bleeding on my boat!"

I thought this old man had a lot of steam when I met him an hour before at the Puako boat ramp. I pulled in to check the tide before going to work. He was launching the boat and had a new convertible Mustang for a tow car. I was interested in the boat and started asking questions. My wife started talking to his wife. Women talking are like listening to jazz. It is all the same song. They can pick up the beat when they meet or if they have been gone, long.

We stepped the mast, and felt out the rigging. I told him I was in the Navy. So was he. I told him I had heard these boats were dangerous for two reasons. First, they will knock you unconscious if they flip over and one of those fiberglass hulls hits you. Second, they can sail away without you. A monohull left unattended will turn up-wind and stop. A Hobie left unattended will trim itself and sail faster without you.

"That's true. My son-in-law and I rented one on Waikiki and almost drowned. The wind came up and we lost it. They rescued us with jet-skis. We rented one on this island and it went so fast it broke apart. Right out there." He pointed to a stretch of ocean about three miles off. He was tired of used-up rental boats and had bought this new one. It was a beauty; black, anodized aluminum wings, and cross members with orange hulls. It had his trademark tequila sunrise sails. Panels of yellow, orange, and red, rose to a red feather on the masthead.

It set bobbing in the shallow water next to the ramp. It drew less than six-inches with the rudders up. I asked, "Where is your crew?"

"It's just me."

"Isn't your wife going with you?"

"No. These things scare her to death."

I said, "Bill, you should have bought a 14-footer. Those you can single hand. This takes two men to right. What if you blow over?"

"I bought this one so my son and son-in-law could go with me."

"Where are they?"

"California."

The women came over and agreed that I should go out with him, just in case something happened. The wind was blowing 10 to 15 knots onshore. Perfect conditions, once you were past the coral reef. Buoys mark a channel for motorboats that can steer through it. We more or less tacked across the deep water and ended up in the shoals. He manned the mainsheet and I juggled the jib. I used a paddle to push us away from the rocks and coral heads. His steering efforts led us into irons a couple of times and we back-pushed the sail to change our azimuth.

Once in deep water he set the traveler for a beam reach, and pulled tight the sail. We took off. It felt like flooring the pedal on a dragster. The acceleration was amazing. We paralleled the shore, a quarter mile off, at the fastest point of sail. We were moving.

The boat was going fast enough to make its own wind. We shifted our weight to keep the Hobie balanced. The rudders hummed. Bill is a speed freak. He wanted to go faster.

"How do we do that?"

"We fly the hull." He told me where to stand, and how to hold on. We gave it a try. I realized, after most of the pain went away, that I was too far forward. We tried it again, and this time I was far enough back to stand over his shoulders. We made it rise up and scream. He found the perfect place between flipping over and falling down and made it fly. He rocketed it on the edge for miles.

We covered a lot of water, and then I had to go to work.

"Head for that beach over there. I have to go to work."

"You work in that hotel?"

"Yes."

"That's where I live. I have a house on the fairways."

"Hey that is great. You can go sailing anytime you want."

He looked at me wearing shorts and blood, barefoot and sunburned. "You can go to work like that?"

"Sure. I have my locker key. I have a towel and there is a shower. My uniform, and shoes are there. I just put it on and punch in."

"Won't they say anything about you just walking up from the beach like that?"

"Fuck'em if they can't take a joke." This became his line, and anytime we were shut out he would use it.

He sailed up the white sand next to the bar. We spun that cat around and I helped him launch. He lowered the rudders in about three feet of water and tacked out three miles to where the wind really blows. I watched his red sail skip across the horizon until sunset. I was hooked. I had to have one.

The next day Bill came by the bar and asked, "Hey, you want to be in a race on Saturday?"

"Where at?"

"Kona: The Kona Sailing Club is having a regatta and I want to kick their ass."

"Okay."

"How is your back?"

"Well, I feel more like I do now, than I did." He laughed. I asked him, "How come you go so far out? Wouldn't it be safer closer to shore?"

Bill pointed out to sea. "You see that line where the white caps go from apart to solid?"

"Yeah."

"That's the wind line caused by the mountains behind us. You get past that and the winds are stronger and steadier. You also want deep water under your hulls. If you flip over in close you can get your mast stuck in the reef and be in real trouble."

I begged the day off and rode my motorcycle down to his place Saturday morning. He admired the bike very much and took a long time asking questions. Then we put the top down on his Mustang and towed the 16 to Honokohau harbor. The starting line for this race was in Kailua Bay. For crowd control, and parking, the ramp was closed at the pier and all boats had to launch at the harbor some five miles north.

We were late getting there, and wasted more time fitting a new red feather to the masthead, and rigging a skull and crossbones flag. There was no wind. A motor launch towed the few multihulls without motors to the starting line. We missed that. I paddled us out of the harbor, past the charter fishing boats, and private yachts. The waves were rolling in the mouth at four-feet, general swells. I paddled up them and about 50 feet off shore we found the faintest of breezes. Rather than exploit this and follow the towboat close in, Bill kept a close haul and worked our way farther out. It took forever to make a quarter mile, then a half. At a mile off we hit the wind line. Bill sheeted out and set a broad reach. We ran for the pier.

As we cleared the last point of land, and turned in, the Ready Flag went up on the judge's boat. It signaled five minutes before the start. We crossed the starting line and headed into the pack. Bill swung it around and threaded through a tangle of yachts. He was pointed the right way when the cannon fired. Out of nowhere came a gust of wind at 35 knots. Bill moved back on the rear corner. I stood over him. He yanked the mainsheet and the Hobie hiked up on one hull. With the sail lifting off the water a scant ten-degrees, we held the breeze and shot out the gate like a raped ape. We left the competition in our wake.

The committee boat was four miles out. We close hauled and headed for a point north of it. The current pushed us south as we worked our way west. Bill kept it trimmed. I kept it balanced. He shoved his feet under the hiking straps and worked the mainsail. Bill held the hiking bar and steered. I stood over him and leaned back holding onto my shroud, and a jib line. I rocked back and forth on the balls of my feet to the rhythm of the ocean. The hull was eight feet over the water and the only sound was the screaming of what little was left of one rudder giving us the barest of steerage.

We held this for a half-hour and I walked taller for days. We were supposed to pass the committee boat's stern and make a right turn for a buoy eight miles off the Kona International Airport. We were so far ahead that Bill made two circles around the boat. Plenty of time for them to record his sail numbers, notice his colors and Jolly Roger and recognize him as the leader. It was his way of registering for the race.

We set sail for the second leg and flew the hull again. The farther we were from land the stronger and more reliable the wind. We shot across the tops of four-foot seas. Hobie Cats are wet boats. We were splashed with spray; the wind tugged our hair; the sun beat on our skin and took the chill out of the wind. I looked behind us and didn't see another sail. I couldn't see the town of Kailua-Kona. We were so far out all I could see was the green of the coffee fields above the town.

Bill started bitching. "Those turds they piss me off. They don't know how to race. They're all back there in a pack having beers and barbecues. You know what's going to happen? They are all going to hit that buoy at sunset and the wind's going to quit. Everybody who doesn't have motor will have to be towed in. You can't win if you are towed in. We have made our point, haven't we?"

"Of course, Bill."

"I mean we have this race in the bag. There isn't anyone even close. We don't have to play these games." And with that he spun the craft around and headed for shore. We pancaked down on both hulls. He let the main swing to one side of the mast and I set the jib on the other. Wing and wing we headed for the harbor. Running with the wind is the calmest point of sail. There is no wind, no sound and no feeling of movement. The only way to tell you are moving is by looking back at the white lines the rudders make in the herringbone wake.

We stretched out on each side of the trampoline and used our life jackets for pillows. As we silently slipped home I asked, "So, how did you make all your money?"

"My parents were into iron and steel."

"Mining or manufacturing?"

"Neither. My mother would iron and my father would steal!"

At sunset rather than be eight miles off and becalmed, everything was secure and we sat around his pool and drank beer. That's what I like about Bill, he is always thinking.

I kept my eye out for a boat and found a 14-footer in Kawaihae with a "For Sale" sign on it. It was well-faded yellow with a white trampoline and sail. The Frenchman who owned it wanted $800. I handed him eight one hundred dollar bills. He gave them back and had seller's remorse. I listened to his adventures on it and asked him about the stains on the trampoline.

"That's fish blood. It won't come out."

"You fished off this thing?"

"I tried. I hooked more fish than I landed. I only caught two."

"What's the problem?"

"The problem is trolling speed is ten-knots. That is 14 miles-an-hour. If you are going 14 miles-an-hour on a Hobie Cat, you are fighting for your life. You have no time to fight a fish."

The trailer didn't have any lights. I mentioned this and he said, "This is Hawaii. You don't need any lights. I will pay your tickets for the first year. How's that?"

He showed me all the parts, gave me the book and sold me the boat. I used a Volkswagen Beetle for a tow car and eventually put lights on the trailer. Hauling it around all the time and stepping the mast each time I sailed was a drag. I needed a place to keep it with the mast up. I asked the manager of the hotel if I could leave it on the beach. He suggested the Cooks' Quarters. The cooks lived in four cedar houses on a rocky point a mile from the hotel. A gulch emptied into the ocean next to the houses and there was a small sandy beach.

It took an afternoon with the cooks and a rented chain saw to cut back the Keawe trees and make a place for it. We ended up with eleven fence posts, which we sold to cover the cost of the saw and buy beer. Bill gave me a set of wheels to prop under the hulls to help drag the boat up the beach. I could tie it well up from the water and the cooks were there to keep an eye on it. I made a box on the trailer to hold the equipment and left a bare boat in the gulch.

Bill sold the 16 and bought a 14 with all the bells and whistles. This new one was a twin for the bigger one. It had orange hulls, black aluminum wings and cross members and tequila sunrise sail. He kept his on the hotel beach and defied anyone to say anything about it. Some people didn't like it but I thought it added a lot of dignity to the shoreline.

I worked a four-hour day in the summer from 10:00 to 2:00. Bill would be launching as I left the bar. I would ride my motorcycle to the Cook's Quarters, pull what I needed out of the box, store my leathers in it, and sail out to meet him. We went sailing every afternoon. We would chase barges, sail around yachts, freighters, and tugs, and play cat and mouse chasing each other for miles, with no fences and no limits.

My boat was so slow compared to his. It had been a rental boat and was used up. They would fill the hulls half full of water to slow the tourists down. All this extra weight took its toll on the fasteners. It was sloppy and walked through waves creaking and groaning with the hulls moving against each other. I took the trampoline off to have new hiking straps sewn on. Bill picked up one hull and walked it six-inches forward without the other hull moving. It was that loose. "We have to do something about this."

Bill had connections with the local Coast Guard Station. One Saturday, when no officers were around, we towed it down there. Those sailors made a jig for it in their shop, out of wood. They measured everything and made it square and then dismantled the boat. Using wire brushes they cleaned all the joints. They brushed on a secret primer and pulled out a gallon of Devcon. It's what the Navy uses to make tools underwater. It's 80% aluminum powder and 20% resin. They mixed up a batch and used putty knives to smear it on the pieces of the aluminum frame and in the joints before rejoining them.

The original rivets were stretched in their holes. The Coasties had oversize rivets and hydraulic guns. They popped them in. It pulled the joints tight and any divots were squeezed full with Devcon. After 24 hours of setting in the jig, four of us carried it outside. We stood it on each corner and spun it. We dropped it on the lawn right side-up and upside-down. We pushed on it and pulled it and placed it back in the jig. It fit perfectly.

We towed it back to my house and put it on sawhorses upside down in the carport. Coast Catamaran had published the templates for the hull specifications in their magazine *The Hobie*

Hotline. I glued them to thin pieces of plywood and took them to the local guitar maker. He cut them out on his band saw.

Bob, the surfer, spent two days working his magic with wax paper, masking tape and plastic resin. He restored the hulls to factory specs and then added knife-edges.

The trampoline came back from the shop just as we finished making oversize rigging. Bill kept the smaller parts of the old rigging, all the pins, shackles, chain plates, and broken ends.

We put it all together and took it down to the harbor. The wind was blowing 25 and gusting to 35 knots. The seas were rolling in. Waves were crashing over the seawall. I told Bill, "Maybe we ought to wait for a better day."

"You pussy!" he roared. "We couldn't ask for a better day for sea trials. The worst that can happen is you die. No one gets out of life alive."

We launched and ate up the harbor. As we headed into the surf and up the ship channel, the hulls pointed up and over the swells rather than walking through them. The noise was gone, and the boat was rigid. The rigging kept the mast from banging around and the sail could adjust quicker and drive harder. It was better than a new boat.

We cleared the outer marker and set a beam reach along the seawall. There was a wall of green water on the port side eight feet high, and one on the starboard side the same. They rolled under us and crashed on the rocks. We couldn't see over the water or through it, but we could see what was below. The coral reef, black lava rocks, areas of deep water floored by sand and fish of all sizes passed in review. There were eels and rays and turtles. It was a cloudy day and with the wind shrieking above us was spooky. I asked Bill, "You come here often?"

"First time. Say, do you hear something?"

We were traversing a trough with just enough cloth aloft to blow us forward. The white hull of a fishing boat crossed our bow. It was cutting across the crests of the waves. We looked up speechless and saw the bottom of the main part of the trawler fill the gap and pass with the bridge and flying bridge. Then came the transom and the lower units of the twin engines with the props spinning and dripping water. The craft roared past and just cleared our mast. Bill didn't look so good. "First time I have seen that, too."

"This sucks!" I intoned, and slackened sail and headed for a secluded beach. As we ran in the swells calmed, and it wasn't so rough. The beach was in sight and on impulse I looked back and saw a 20-foot wave towering over the mast. Flecks of foam fell from its crest. Before I could yell, "Golly Bill!" the wave broke and all hell with it. Someone poured 50 gallons of water in each ear. The boat flooded and we were pushed under water.

I looked at Bill. He was holding on to the hiking straps with both hands. His cheeks were swelled with air and it was four-feet of water over his head to daylight. His hat was still on with a blank expression under it. I was holding my breath. I had the mainsheet line in one hand, the tiller in the other.

We popped up like the proverbial cork. The white water drained. I turned around and steered up the coming, larger, wave. We made it almost to the top and started to fall back on the face of the wave. Bill scrambled out on one bow and I did the other. We held on and kept it pointed up as the wave broke beneath us. The cat fell into it. We were swamped, but not submerged. All the weight was forward and like monkeys in a sidecar we crawled back and got set for the next one. I grabbed the tiller and steered up the third wave. The helm was sluggish but it kept us pointed up and over. Bill was a hood ornament.

The port rudder had broken off during our trip to the bottom. A rock or coral head had snapped it clean, just below the boss. With its loss it was an hour climbing over waves and crawling into the wind to get back to the harbor.

After we had loaded it on the trailer and tied it down, Bill handed me $15.00. It was half the cost of a new rudder. Shipmates do that.

The boat didn't break and it was fast. Bill couldn't catch it. We would swap boats and I couldn't catch it. Bill made every improvement to his boat and still couldn't catch it. The secret was in the rigid hulls, the rigging and the sail. The old white sail was covered with orange tell-tales. It looked like it was used for wind studies, and it was. If the nylon streamers point up, pull the tiller tight. If they point down, let off ever so slightly. If they stream straight back, hold your course. Your direction doesn't matter if you are far enough out. Practice obtaining maximum boat speed. Stand on a flying hull for as many minutes as you can and study the streamers on the sail.

We played all summer long, three miles off. We entered every race in Kawaihae. Bill wouldn't go back to Kona. They were too genteel for him. He preferred the bang and board, cut-throat racing of the crazies in Kawaihae, where no one protested the collisions at the start and everybody was too tired to party afterwards.

While the other crews had their boats on the trailers waxing the hulls for speed, I would be up to my nipples in sea water rubbing mine with a worn out piece of 600 grit sandpaper. It was a rat boat with faded yellow hulls and orange patches. I shot some gray primer on it for affect. It was never waxed. Wax melts in the sun and leaves pockets in the finish that create drag.

When the horn sounded it would glide across the top of the water and out gun all the other 14's and pass some of the 16-footers. It couldn't catch the leading 16's or the 18'. Hull length determines overall boat speed. The 18' was so fast it was the judge's boat, the committee boat, and the winner.

Bill would be somewhere in the back passing larger yachts as he came out. Any newcomer he passed he would toss a piece of old rigging aboard. In a few minutes someone would take it to the captain and he would hove to while the crew checked every fitting on the boat. If they couldn't find it below they would send someone aloft. This distracted them from the race and gave everyone else an advantage. Bill is ornery like that.

I was on the third leg coming in when I passed Bill heading out. He was blown over and using two trash bags full of water belted around his neck to pull it up. He didn't weigh 150 pounds and this was an emergency. I offered to help, but he waved me on. I was winning and there were other boats headed his way. He would stop one of them and slow down the competition. This old man risks his life alone in a 16 and he can't even right a 14. Watch out for old guys. They have nothing to lose.

In 20 minutes I was in and across the finish line. I turned around and headed out to help Bill. By then he was up and sailing. I provided escort.

Bill is always searching for the perfect wave to park his hull on and run across the wind. He knows when to quit and when to head in. One evening we crossed a beautiful white yacht. It was so smooth and sleek, and the rigging was almost invisible. We sailed around it, talking, and admiring it. The owner came up on deck. He proved to be a bore with a beard.

He intimated he was richer than both of us, put together, and we were invading his privacy and get the hell out of his view. Bill could have bought and sold this jerk. Instead he apologized and we sailed away. As he crossed the stern, and out of sight of the owner, he reached up and silently slipped a piece of chain plate on the deck.

We sailed for years. Our wives had a standing order. If we aren't back in three days call the Coast Guard. When my dermatologist told me to stay out of the sun, there went the fun. But if you would like to go, Bill is waiting. He is three miles off where the wind is willing. His is the red sail in the sunset.

SKIPPY

"Do you like peanut butter?"

"Well, my name is Skippy," and he gets a laugh. He drinks light beer on ice with a straw. He is in his 40's, single, rather big for his size, and writes jokes. He travels with his father and uncle. The three of them make a Jokers Wild. His father writes children's books. His uncle writes letters to the editor. Skippy writes my jokes on cocktail napkins, and stuffs them in his hat. He tips his hat to the ladies and chases the napkins down the sidewalk in the wind. Little kids help him. Everybody knows Skippy.

He wears aloha shirts, shorts, and deck shoes. He goes around the world and mails me jokes written on napkins from far away bars. His jokes are clean and for little kids. He wears a beaded belt, like a big brother. He is best with the young.

"Hey, buddy. What did one sesame seed say to the other? We are on a roll," and he gets a laugh. He doesn't drink like he did, and I am glad he quit smoking. He wants to go on a motorcycle ride across America with me. I wouldn't risk his hide on a ride and suffer the wrath of his father, or his uncle. They play golf in the mornings and games with balls on the lawn, in the setting sun. It looks like fun. Skippy spends three months on the grounds, the dead of winter. When spring comes he renews his quest to find the best jokes for his pals, his buddies.

He did a whole series on bees. Why he picks on bugs eludes me. He will rattle them off and when he doesn't get a laugh, presses on with, "Okay, how about this one?" and comes up with more. When Bud began putting born-on dates on their beer, Skippy began putting born-on dates on his jokes.

He loves it when people cherish him and just a little attention really gets him going. He is funny, and when he doesn't make it to the bar he is missed. His public asks for him and his presence over the years has made him a part of the entertainment.

I've had him and his relatives, when it was late, rocking the bar with laughter. We sift jokes quickly with a first line and a punch line. If all know the joke we move on to another. If one hasn't heard the joke, the person who remembers it tells it. We laugh so hard, that we cry and our sides ache. These are the friends you make, behind bars.

In a weak moment Skippy told me about the day he ran away from home. He packed a suitcase in each hand, balanced a canoe on his head, and left. He had a book of matches in one pocket for survival. His knife, which he had spent the better part of the day before sharpening, was weighing down the other.

He wasn't gone three minutes when he was missed. His father held back his mother, at the back door, and watched him trundle down the road. The going was slow. The day was warm. He left the road and cut across the fields to the river. Twice he dropped the canoe. It was hurting his head. He would have left it behind, but it was essential to his plan.

His father's study was a cupola on the roof of a two-story farmhouse. It was glass all around and had a view like an air-control tower. He looked over farms and fields, to the horizon, in all directions. It was where he felt inspired to write. Today his attention was drawn to the river, and to his first born, Skippy, who was doing something new.

Skippy dropped the canoe for the last time and sat down in the shade on the riverbank. The brown water rushing by made him feel cooler. He was winded, and wondering if he had enough stuff. He didn't want to carry anymore. He loaded what he had in the boat and was ready to launch, when he had second thoughts. He realized he was leaving a lot behind.

Then he noticed the trees all around him were chewed through. There where white chips all around the bases of the trees. Some trees were lying on the ground, still attached to a stump only a foot high. He looked closer at the stump and noticed teeth marks. Something in his brain screamed, "BEAVERS." He was scared now. Without realizing it, he jumped in the canoe and began paddling furiously. He shot into the current and was carried down stream at about 19 knots.

His father had been watching with binoculars, and wasn't worried, until now. His mother had been calmed down, and was downstairs in the kitchen, looking out the window, and expecting regular reports from the tower. Before the father could make a sound, Skippy ran aground. There was a small island in the middle, and he had been heading for it all along.

He lugged his suitcases up in the shade of some scrub. He tugged the canoe completely out of the water. Then, he took a break. He looked at the water separating him from both sides and felt cool. He laid back and checked out the sky. He didn't see any birds or airplanes flying by.

He felt ready to move in. He pulled out his knife and walked down the beach looking for beavers. He didn't expect to find any because there weren't any trees. Trees are slow to grow and floods washed them away small.

He walked around the island, and then across the middle. It was sand hills and driftwood, and weeds and grass. It had a beach, and he was the only one on it. There was a stand of tamarack bushes. Their long whip branches were just right for his shelter. He started cutting wood. The green wood was tough. He made it tougher by cutting straight across it.

When he had a pile, he pulled it in the shade and stripped the leaves and small branches. With these, he sharpened the ends and drove them into the sand. He used more to lace in the walls and make a roof. He ended up with a three-sided box that he could sit in, and be out of the wind.

All this activity made him hungry. He had a peanut butter sandwich and a pickle in his suitcase. He didn't want to eat that, because it was dinner. He sat in his shelter and realized he had better go fishing. He remembered seeing some line on some tumbleweeds, and a hook and lure not far away. He scavenged some tackle and using a sharp stick dug up half the island looking for a worm.

He found one worm, and one hook, and about 15 feet of line. He tied it on the longest branch he could find, tossed it in the river and caught a bush. He worked hard to put it all together and he was mad. He yanked the line with all he was about, and brought out a trout. It was hooked on its dorsal fin.

The fish was small, but it was enough. He cleaned it and made a fire. He put it on a stick and cooked it, dropped it, got it covered with ashes, blew them off and ate it. He ate part of it; he was afraid of swallowing a bone. The rest he buried.

He divided his time between lying in the sun and daydreaming, and walking around looking for treasure. He studied his hut and would add a branch or two. He was getting a blister on his thumb from all the cutting. He sat and watched the water.

About sundown his father went to collect him. He came home sunburned, and scratched up. He had mosquito bites. His clothes were dirty. He had a full day.

GEORGE

George is Japanese. He was born in America, but his parents weren't. The old people came in the 1920's to California, to labor on the farms as immigrant workers. They stuck together, worked hard, were frugal and by the late 30's owned their own farms and oceanfront property. After Pearl Harbor, December 7, 1941, his family lost everything, except what they could carry to the train heading for Arizona.

The first day in the relocation camp was hectic. All pitched in just to get a meal together. George was nine years old. There was a horse tied to a rail. It was saddled and wore a bridle. He petted it and became fast friends. He grabbed the reins and jumped aboard. He was surprised how wide the animal was. Just like in the comics, he kicked it and raced across the desert. With the wind in his hair and low hills in an orange sun as his target, he rode on.

His weight was nothing for the roan. She ran as if alone, in a long arc and then back to the buildings. It was hot, and white sweat was beginning to foam around the saddle. George thought this was all right. There was nothing like this back home: the smell of the horse, the new plants and the relief from the dread his parents had felt all day.

The owner of the horse was waiting by the rail. George rappelled down after hooking the reins over the horn. He pulled them loose and tied them around the post. The cowboy said, "Son, do you know they still hang horse-thieves in Arizona?" George was in shock. "But because of your young age, and you just got here and probably didn't know that, I am going to let it go this one time. But, don't you ever take a man's horse again."

He laughs about it now. The experience made an impression on him that is with him still. He was finally awarded a settlement from the government for the treatment. He uses it for a scholarship fund to help kids of Japanese ancestry go to college.

George is successful. He works hard, is frugal, never forgets what the family has been through, and honors his parents in all things. He made millions as an engineer-contractor putting buildings and parking lots on that oceanfront property taken from them 20 years before.

His wife died after giving him two daughters, 10 years apart. He never remarried, so the first girl raised the second one. The first girl became a rocket scientist; the second teaches math on a college level. Neither one is married and I tell them you are never going to find a guy at those Mensa meetings. To number one I say, "You are pushing 40. Lower your standards." To number two I say, "Don't look for a husband. Look for a single man."

They vacation together, and the sight of them coming my way brings joy to my day. We have watched each other grow up, and noticed the change in hair color and the deepening of the crow's feet. George has a ready laugh. He gets the joke. He complains that he can't tell a joke, but he does okay. He sings when he has been drinking. He embarrasses his daughters and they tell him, "This not a Karaoke Bar." Even that gets a laugh.

As a regular customer, he always brings me jokes. I remember his jokes, because I remember him. His signature joke is called Patrick O'Flannery's Laundry.

An Irishman is traveling across the West and in a small town he comes across Patrick O'Flannery's Laundry painted on a building. Thinking he will visit with a countryman he goes inside. There is a little Chinaman running the laundry. He asks, "How did you ever come up the name Patrick O'Flannery?"

"Well," said the owner, "when I first came to this country I was standing in Customs and Immigration. I think there was a Patrick O'Flannery ahead of me in line. The man with the clipboard was asking, 'Where are you from? Where did you go to school? Have you ever been arrested? What do you do for a living?' Then he turns to me and asks, 'What's your name?' I said, 'Sam Ting.'"

George was with me the night the hotel closed for an 18-month remodel. It was July 10. Liz and Diesel where there. He is a drummer. She is a local lady. I was closing and they talked about the end of an era. No one knew what the new Japanese owner was going to do with the place. Some said condos; some said it was staying closed. All was conjecture trying to second-guess the oriental mind.

A big bash was set up on North lawn. There were lights and bands and pavilions full of food and drink. All the beautiful people were milling about enjoying the night air. We watched it from the beach, wondering if we would ever see anything so grand again. I opened a cabinet to put some booze away and a dozen pop-bottle rockets fell out in my hand. The Security Guards had confiscated them on the Fourth of July holiday.

The hotel has a policy of no fireworks by the guest as a public safety. The resort provides pyrotechnics on some holidays or at a group's request. It takes permits and special people with bomb-carrying trucks and advance notice, and lots of money.

I gave each of them an empty wine bottle, three rockets and a book of matches. We walked down the dark beach. We buried our bottles, angled out to sea, inserted a rocket and lit it. Three soared, but George's was a no-show. Liz ran down to help him and this time three more went. She ran back to her bottle and using whispered calls we managed to light four at once. George lit his last one. It was perfect. We pulled our bottles out of the sand and hurried back to the bar.

We almost made it. Two Security Guards came racing down the steps to the beach. They were at the foot of the stairs when I started yelling. "You guests give me those bottles. You know you are not supposed to do that." Waving the bottles at the guards I shouted, "It's okay guys. I have them. They won't do it again." They waved, turned back up the stairs, and went back towards the party.

It was a close call. Never underestimate the power of a Security Guard. It was a rent-a-cop that brought down a President. A guy, just doing his low-paying job, caught the plumbers in the Watergate Building.

George keeps coming back. He fishes off the rocks and visits the graves of those he loves.

THE ROCK

If you have to work anyway you might as well hang out at a nice bar. I work on the best beach on the planet. It is rated number one, every five years by the travel magazines. The sand is soft and warm. The water changes from clear to royal blue. It is 83 degrees and gradually gets deep with no rocks under your feet. It is one-fifth of a mile long, crescent-shaped and backed by palms growing from the lawns. It is everyone's calendar-perfect-picture of Hawaii. There is an elegant hotel hidden in the trees and the tropical breezes are embracing. The most beautiful women work here and the gentlest men.

Island people are talented. They can sing and dance, play musical instruments, weave, build, sew, carve, craft, plant, reap, fish, and smile while they are at it. Any fiefdom would be lucky to have an island population.

The guests are the best. They are well dressed, well oiled, well heeled, and well off. The rocks on their fingers cost more than my house. The economy doesn't bother them. True wealth is when you can live off the interest on the interest. The ups and downs of the stock market, and the whims of fortune lost have no affect on them. If it does, they are not our customers. They are well educated, well behaved, and well secured. If we are out of something, it doesn't bother them. They will have something else. They are not like the mom-and-pop tourists who save all their lives for one trip to Honolulu, and expect a $1.50 back for every dollar spent.

It is a day shift. You don't have to wash glasses. Everything is in plastic. No glass around bare feet. The windows are always clean, because there aren't any. It doesn't smell like a bar. The beaches are lined with peaches. The money is good. The other guys have three jobs to make what this bar pays. It is the top of the heap, the epitome of bar tending gigs. It is a high wire and you work without a net.

The hotel is like a cruise ship plowing northwest at the rate of one-inch a year, (continental drift) and we are the dinghy. The captain is in his cabin and the palace politics are up the ladder. We are down here bobbing with the paying customers. The boss forgets we're here until we do something unforgettable.

All this, and the best part of the day is riding a motorcycle to work. Out on the highway clipping along at slightly faster than the fastest car. Never let a car pass you when you are on a motorcycle. Find a section of road and settle in with nothing behind you and nothing in sight. Always hang on to the controls. Never stand on a peg. Pegs can break off.

Read the road or drop it. Watch out for wet spots on the road. Avoid leaves and sand, painted strips and gravel in the corners. Look past manhole covers so you don't hit them. Your tire goes where your eye sees. If you imagine you will hit a rock in the road, you will. Any time there is a confrontation between the imagination and the will, the imagination wins.

Avoid target fixation. It can kill you. If your eyes are locked on the apex of a turn you have hit too fast, pry them off the spot, and look down the road to where you want to be. Let your reflexes take over. If there is an animal in your path, look down the road, and pick a way around. Plot a line and follow it with your mind. Modern motorcycles are capable of more maneuvers than the average human can hang on for. Target fixation is deadly for skydivers. They become so focused on where to land they forget to pull the ripcord.

Do not abdicate control. Riding it into the ground is not an option. You must practice riding on the edge. Hit corners so fast the front tire slips and the rear one spins, and slide it through. It is amazing what bikes will do. You must lean them to turn them; forget turning the handlebars; pull away from the direction of the lean, and push down into it. If the apex is closing faster, you must lean further, and force yourself to push it more. It's called counter-steering. If you have been doing it all along, don't worry about it.

The road to the job runs 20 miles by the sea. Going down, the ocean is on the right and the Kohala Mountains on the left. The three tall mountains, Hualalai, Mauna Loa and Mauna Kea rise big and blue, and beckon you. The ocean has a few boats and a few whales, and little to block the view. The blacktop drops from 600 feet to sea level, through the foothills of Mahukona and then the desert scrub to Kawaihae. It is two lanes of less-traveled, well-paved, and little-trafficked, county road.

The ride back is along the Alenuihaha Channel, the second roughest stretch of water in the world. The island of Maui takes up the view. It rises out of the ocean and gets bigger as you climb back to Hawi, where the debris meets the sea.

The reflectors glued to the road's surface are called Bott's dots. They reflect the way at night. There is a row of red on the left, yellow down the middle, and white on the right. These are necessary because it gets cave-like dark in Hawaii. Once you get around the corner from the lights of Kawaihae, it looks like the stars are touchable. Hawaii is the farthest place on the planet from an inhabited continent. You cannot get any farther away. This separation from all that light makes it the best place for stargazing. If there is a new moon and many clouds, it is so dark you can't see your hand in front of your face.

The good news is the lights on motorcycles are better than ever. They use Halogen bulbs that put out enough lumens to blister the paint on a stop sign. The bad news is we all march to the tune of a different bummer.

The shift is from noon until dark. Last call is sunset. Look for the green flash. That's me leaving. Some motorcycles love high gear. It is better to ride a slow motorcycle fast, than a fast motorcycle slow.

I was cruising home well after dark. At ten miles over the limit and leaning into the wind I was passed by a white Toyota station wagon. The car pulled right in front of the bike. The headlight was shining on the chrome bumper. I was thinking, "Wow, how about a little room?" when a rock the size of a watermelon came from between the rear wheels. As soon as I saw it, I hit it.

Back on the ranch we had a horse called WM, for Widow Maker. It was his habit to buck off the first rider every morning. If you were late leaving the bunkhouse then WM was the only horse left in the remuda. We would never put a woman on this animal, but if some kid from town came out to show us how it was done, we would arrange him a flight. As soon as you were seated, he would rise up and bow and kick in one fast motion. You expected it and instinctively wrapped the stirrups around his belly and held on to the saddle horn with both hands. There is a second of loading, then weightlessness and finally settling down. After he tried it, he would work for you all day. You could get off and on him ten times and he wouldn't do it again.

This isn't the rodeo. There isn't anyone around to impress. You are still expected to work all day. So you hang on with all you've got. And what killed the cowboys? Accidents with animals is what. If your horse bucks you off in the middle of nowhere and breaks your leg and runs away, you are in trouble. Don't take any chances with these animals.

I know the feeling of being bucked off and got a grip on the bars. The front tire banged the boulder and the bike flew into the air. The back tire topped it and trimmed the flight. It bounced hard. I came down over the instruments, helmet on the front fender with my face in the headlight. I was looking down at the highway, still doing 60 miles an hour, at the line where the pavement ends and the gravel begins. I was wondering where to start sliding, and where to stop.

Wishing to slow down, I found my hands were still on the grips. My feet were still on the pegs. I pushed myself up and sat on the gas cap. The seat is on a sub-frame that sticks out over the back wheel. I hoped it was still there as I slid back off the tank. It was. The bike had taken a shot. I wanted to stop and look it over. As it slowed to 50 mph the tachometer and speedometer began to hula and were hard to focus on. The grips kept trying to slap the tank. I sped back up to 65 mph and decided to deal with it later.

It was 15 miles to Hawi and just me on the road. The car was gone. I wished he would have stayed in the passing lane and honked his horn, so I would have noticed that stone. He pulled in quick to miss it and set me up. The safest thing you can do as a motorcyclist is to drive a car and look out for other motorcyclists.

If you were standing in line at the Hawi Theater for the movie that evening, it was I on the street doing the watusi with a motorcycle. After five miles of holding on at 35 mph my arms felt like lead. Turning was like steering a wheelbarrow full of Jell-O. I rolled it into Arizona, the dehumidified room where I keep it, and my wife looked at me. I was white as a ghost and she said, "I worry about you on that damn thing."

I told her the story and inspected the bike. The front hub had fragmented. Four spokes were adrift and flagging the broken pieces. The front wheel was caved. Amazingly the tire hadn't gone flat. It had a tube and wasn't torn. The back wheel was caved, although not as bad. Bummer. The good news is that anywhere in the world, you are only ten days away from Honda parts.

I laid the wheels on the parts counter in Kona and the clerk cried. "These wheels look like new; it's a shame to bend them." He couldn't believe the wheels were so old. I explained where the bike is kept, and that it is only washed in gravity flow rainwater. No high pressure and no minerals. He said he gets wheels half this old that are trashed. We agreed that paradise is hard on things. The sun, salt, and sand never stop moving. The moisture and the toxins from the volcano gang up on metal. He was surprised I didn't drop the bike and this was the only damage. I have been his customer for 20 years and this event earned a new appraisal.

In ten days I had new wheels. It was 30 days before the mechanic found three hours to be alone with them and get them trued. They work like new. The first time I ran out of gas, the gas cap wouldn't open. My using it for a seat locked it tight. It took some minutes of panic, lubricant and tension to make it useable.

Rocks come in all sizes and if you are on a bike at night never stop looking for them.

THE RIVER

It was one of those years when the news said Colorado was flooding, but it wasn't. Sure the river was up to the road in places, and on some of the curves in the canyons, you might get your wheels wet. The roads were open and there was no traffic. It was the year the mountain man shot the sheriff, and they had manhunts all over South Park. The Arkansas River was at its highest point in 20 years. We drove along it and marveled at the trees and houses, trash and horses that floated by. It wasn't raining. The water was all snowmelt. It had been a bad winter and now the sun of summer was filling creek and stream, and feeding the river.

It was my brother-in-law's idea to float down the river. He's an ex-river guide and claimed it was more fun than Disneyland. "How did you break your back, Joe?" I asked.

"Oh, that was at the end of the day, putting the boat away. That didn't happen on the river." He persuaded us that this was the safest time ever because the river was so high. "It's well above all the rocks and it's going faster than usual, so you get a good ride," he said. "There have been times when the river was so low, we all had to get out and turn the boat on its side and walk to deeper water."

"I don't know, Joe. When I was a kid they told us to stay away from the river. We were barred from it."

"Well white water rafting is big business. And usually you have to book in advance and take a number. But now, because of the bad press and lack of tourists, you can go anytime." He opened another beer and continued with, "The best way is to take an oar boat. That way you have a guide who knows the river, handles the oars, and controls the boat. The other option is a paddleboat, where everybody has a paddle and pulls together. I have been on some paddleboats that I wanted to just walk away from and leave those people to their own devices. I don't know how they ever got back. They can't take orders, can't take advice, can't take a hint, and haven't got a clue. They all do their own thing and around and around we go." He made a circling motion with his beer can.

He can't be a guide anymore, because of his back, but he loves going down the river. My wife's sister, Carol, loves it too. She's gone 22 times and had nothing but fun. It was her birthday, and she was celebrating getting down to 200 lbs. in Weight Watchers. My wife and daughter's moods ranged from skeptical to ambivalent. Joe's son John, a 16-year-old nephew, was available. A boat seats six.

Joe recommends a company and gives them a call. "We have a group leaving now, if you would like to join us," answers the secretary. We drive down to look it over. We case the office and store, and admire the enlarged photographs of smiling customers on the wall. Everything looks ship shape so we cut a deal with the cashier.

The temperature of the river water is 34 degrees. I insist on wetsuits and boots for my wife, daughter and myself. The other three elect to wear swimsuits under cotton shirts and pants, with sandals. There are changing rooms with lockers. We suit up. The staff takes us out to a shed and puts life vests on us that clamp like vises. "Aren't these a little tight?" I complain.

"You want them tight if you go in the water," says the blonde, Baywatch, striker.

We mill around for 20 minutes in the sun, in black with orange, and perspire, while they load six Zodiac inflatable boats onto a trailer behind an ancient school bus painted blue. We board the bus and ride several miles out of Buena Vista, on the highway towards Salida, then turn off on a dirt road and go a couple more. We arrive at a wide spot in the road with flat area for parking next to the river. All the commercial ventures put in here. The businesses are limited to six boats, in a flotilla. There is a lot of traffic on the river.

We are herded into an area for a safety lecture. There is no shade. The afternoon sun beats down and the tight rubber suits, and tighter life vests, have us stewing in our own juices.

There is a blonde with a clipboard who appears to be the chick in charge. The first point she covers is hypothermia. "The river is two degrees above freezing. If you fall into it, get out of it right away. Keep your eye on your guide. He will either pull you back in the boat or point for you to swim to shore." She relates the figures on how long a person, depending on how they are dressed, can survive the immersion. None of it sounds pleasant.

She continues, "If your boat goes over and you have to swim in the river, do it like you are in an arm chair. Keep your feet out in front of you, lean back and let your life vest keep you afloat. If you get in trouble we will throw you a line. It comes in a bag. Do not grab the bag, because all the line will come out. Grab the line. If you are pulled, either back to the boat or ashore, lie on your back and hold the line on your chest. This keeps you face up in the water. Keep your eye on your guide.

"If your guide has to pull you back into the boat, he may push you under and let the buoyancy of the water help lift you out. Expect this and help him out.

"Do not stand up in the river. If you stand up, the rocks can trap your feet and the current will knock you over, and if you cannot escape, you will drown. The river is very powerful. Do not take chances with it.

"Watch out for strainers. These are places where deadwood and trash have collected on rocks and made piles of debris. Swim away from them. It you can't swim away and are going to hit one, when you come close, crawl on top. If you don't, you will be sucked under and drown.

"Always hold onto the boat. There are straps, handles, oarlocks, and any number of things to hold onto. Hang onto something, because things happen quickly.

"If you are in the water and can breathe, and it is dark, you are under the boat. You must come out from under the boat. You can be dragged over rocks and severely injured. It feels safe under the boat, but you must come out. Listen to your guide.

"Be careful of high sides. If your boat hits a large rock and rides up on one side your guide will call, 'High Side Right' or 'High Side Left'! This means everybody move to that side of the boat and keep it right side up."

The lecture is followed by a summary of commands for the people in the paddleboats, and a period for questions. There aren't many. Most of the people have done it all before, and look rather bored. The big difference is, if you go over in a paddleboat everybody can get back on and paddle it upside down. If you go over in an oar boat, the oars become useless and you are screwed.

We are assigned a boat and take our positions. Our fleet consists of three paddleboats; two oar boats and a trainee. A young lady who wants to be a guide, is taking a Zodiac filled with five-gallon water jugs for ballast, down the river, solo. We push off. My wife and I flank our Daughter Dearest in the bow. Joe and John bookend Carol in the stern.

Our guide, Morgan, sits on a framework of aluminum tubes that stay the oarlocks. He mans the sweeps. His arms are smaller around than the oars. He has long red hair, lots of freckles and blue eyes.

For several minutes, we drift down a wide, muddy, river. We had spent the previous week at Disneyland, where the thrill is controlled. The kid starts complaining, "When does the fun start?" To keep her occupied, we quiz her on the points of the safety lecture. With the memory of youth, she corrects us on things we've skipped. I make sure we all have a strap to hang onto and we float along; glad to be in the cool on the water and the shade of the trees. We study the dynamics of the river, commenting on how the waves break backwards compared to the ocean.

Morgan is a good guide. He maneuvers us down the middle and keeps control of the boat. It is idyllic. We float under a footbridge, and watch the planks pass overhead. He doesn't say much, too young to have a practiced speech. We ask him about this and that. He is serious and reserved, yet pleasant. He steers us around the rocks and it's exciting. The river narrows and makes a right turn into a gorge. After the turn, there is a rock the size of a house, in the middle. The water divides, and funnels into troughs going straight down both sides. We hit the rock, high side, flip over, and go in the water. Visibility turns to zero.

You instinctively hold your breath in a situation like this. It is cold. All your pores slam shut; the shivers start and your arms cling to your sides like those of a baby rat dipped in honey. I feel the strap and look up to the surface. I jerk on it, fearing it will snap loose, and come up behind the boat. I am dragged like a sea anchor. Daughter Dearest pops up next to me still holding her strap. I grab her with my free hand and bring her close to the boat. She is perceptive for a 10-year-old, and with teeth chattering, tells me, "Now I know how an icicle feels."

My wife surfaces next to the kid and loses her strap. I have no hand with which to grab her. She swims a stroke and reaches up and takes a purchase with her index finger in a drain hole.

There must have been a trap door I hadn't noticed, because Morgan comes crawling back and grabs the kid. We hoist her up and then he lifts the wife. I push, and he pulls, and she goes aboard. Then he tells me, "Big Fella, I can't lift you up, back here."

I am thinking, "Tell Laura I love her..."

He says, "You have to let go and come up the side of the boat. I will lift you out there." I let go and am pulled along by the shoulders of the life vest. With the oarlocks at my knees he says, "If you please," and pushes me under water. I rise up and he and the wife haul me aboard. The river roars. We are in a canyon and moving fast. Rocks are all around us.

John swims to the side and Morgan pulls him on. He is worried about his father and starts calling "Dad!" Joe is sucked into a hole. He holds his breath for 40 seconds and crawls up and out, under water, until his flotation can overcome the cavitations. We see his head, in the center of the washing machine, in the path of the trainee. She knocks him under without noticing. He comes up again, and is pulled into a paddleboat bringing up the rear. They put him ashore and he walks along the bank following the action.

Another paddleboat has made the side and wedged itself in the rocks. One of the crew throws a bag of line to Morgan. Like salvation it sails across the water and right into his hands. He grabs the line and holds tight. The boat slows. The guy holding the line lets it go when it begins to run out and burn his hands.

We gather speed and are rushed through the rapids with white water everywhere. It is like raising guavas. You are at the mercy of the juicer.

My wife worries about her sister and asks, "Where is Carol?" We start calling her name and looking at the boats around us. She isn't in any of them. The shrugged shoulders mean no one has seen her. She isn't on either shore.

Suddenly, weakly, we hear, "I am under here. I am under the boat."

Morgan springs into action and asks, "Where are you?"

She answers, "I won't come out."

He smiles, "Just stick one hand out. Let me see your hand." A right hand appears on the starboard side just past the oarlock. Morgan is a smart kid. He motions for us to help. He sees her head raising the fabric on the bottom. In one motion he stomps on her head, grabs her hand, and yanks her out from under the boat. As she slides out, we grab her and lift her aboard. She is bruised, blue, and bleeding. We give her a cursory examination. Nothing seems broken. The wounds aren't deep. The blood is from abrasions. We rest her in the middle of the boat.

We arc in a calm area with a short beach on one side, and a rock wall on the other. Another paddleboat has tied off to a tree. A guide throws a bag of line that is tied to the tree. It crosses our boat and Morgan grabs it. The boat slows and he begins to slide off. I catch his right leg and call to the wife, "Grab his other leg." She holds on to him and the boat. We play stretch the guide. The boat slows more. The line becomes tight. We watch in disbelief as the D-ring in the bag opens. The lines fall in the water. We take off again. We are racing around rocks and past strainers. Ahead is a rock gate, where the river goes in and only noise comes out.

Morgan pushes himself upright and begins coiling the line. You can tell a lot about a sailor by the way he stows his line. He tells us, "There is too much weight on this boat. They can't stop it. You must all swim to shore, now." He points to the beach. A mental calculation comes up with 800 lbs., and I decide he has a point here. However, in Hawaii, on the ocean, the rule is 'Stay with your boat.' Your boat is your lifeline to the land. Before I can bring this up, Daughter Dearest dives in the river. Her cousin John does the same. Both of them begin doing a panic-stricken, Australian crawl stroke. Where that kid goes her mother goes. The wife's dive is shallow and flat. She skips across the water, twice, like a stone, and paces the children.

As I dive in, Carol says, "I can't swim. I am not going."

Morgan assures her, "You are with me."

It is so cold. Every stroke takes concentration. I hit the water and muscle through the icy soup. The hesitation costs me prime real estate when it comes to getting out. I am carried past the beach along a dirt embankment. I frantically pull small pieces of grass and weeds off the bank, denuding the slope, trying to get a grip. I try to stand, but the water is too deep. The limb of a cottonwood tree that is dragging the water catches me. Like an ant I manage to extricate myself by crawling up the branch, and wearily walk back to the crew.

They are stretched out like limp lizards on large rocks. The heat sinks into me off a hot one. I watch the white clouds blow by in the blue sky, and try to remember ever being colder. No one has much to say. Nobody wants to talk to me. It's a sunny afternoon. The air temperature must be 80 degrees.

Presently the chick in charge, with the clipboard, comes up in a boat. She totes a waterproof bag full of wool sweaters. She has us remove the life jackets and put on several sweaters. She takes our vital signs, looks us over, and asks about any injuries. She interviews all of us in turn, and takes copious notes. She is very professional. After an hour of rest and warming up, she announces we are getting in the boats and going around the bend, to check on Carol and rendezvous with the rest of the group.

The kid balks. She tells me, "I don't want to go back in that river."

"I don't either," I confess. "But, we are just going around the bend. Not all the way down the river. Let's go around the bend, check on your aunt Carol and see what these people have to say." The two of us crawl into a paddleboat. By way of breaking the ice I tell the crew, "Hello. I am Crusoe. This is Friday. It is just another shipwreck day."
There are a few smiles. It's a tough crowd.

Six strong paddles are the way to get around on a raging river. You have power. You have control. I mention to the kid, "This is the way to do it; use galley slaves." This group is not amused. They work in unison, with few commands, and put us in a spot of shade with rocks making a natural landing. Our boat has been righted and is tied down stream. The rest of the boats are here. The people wander around and check the flora and fauna.

Carol is stretched on some large rocks well up from the water. They have gone over her with a first-aid kit and she is bandaged and presentable. She is covered with wool sweaters. We file by and all say something. I am last in line so sit down and ask her, "How do you like this? Next year, on your birthday, we are going bull riding." She moans and her eyes roll back in her head. I say, "Don't stare at the sun, dear. It makes people wonder about you."

I give her a neurological check. Using my hand to shield the sun I make sure her pupils react to light and are the same size. I ask her a few questions. "What's your name? What day is this? Where are you?" She is lucid. I tell her I am going to pinch her toes, to make sure she has feeling in them. "Is that okay?"

She says, "Okay," and eyes me suspiciously. I take her pulse. It is thready and weak. "That's my arm."

"Just making sure you weren't waiting for it." I check her toes, fingers, and knee jerk reaction. She has feeling. I can tell she is going to be okay because she starts kidding around.

Carol whispers hoarsely, "Would somebody get this guy away from me?"

The chick in charge taps me on the shoulder and asks, "Are you a doctor?"

"No, a bartender."

She says, "Come with me."

I tell Carol, "I will be right back."

"Don't hurry," Carol, says, stronger now.

We walk out of earshot among the rocks. The chick in charge leads, then stops and turns. I say, "My sister-in-law is in shock. We need to get her the hell out of here."

"Dig it. I'm hip. I may need your help to convince her to get back in the boat," she says.

"She doesn't want to go?"

"No!"

"What are her options?" I inquire.

"She can walk out or she can float out. We are in touch with the people who take the photographs. They are four miles from the end of the ride. They have a radio and we can have a car waiting at the highway. Carol can't walk. We can have her off the river in an hour, if she will get back in the boat."

She has no argument from me, I relent and join up saying, "I'm with you."

We walk back to Carol. The chick in charge has some bedside manner. She kneels down, takes her hand and says, "Carol, how are you doing? We have to get moving. The sun is

going down. Now you can walk out of here, but it is 16 miles to
the road. There is no trail, and you have lost your shoes. Or, you
can get back in the boat and we will have you off the river in one
hour. I will not lie to you. This is the start of the ride. There are
eleven more miles of rapids, and the worst is yet to come. We will
make every effort to get you off this river safely."

Big tears well up in Carol's eyes and run down her cheeks.
She resigns herself and sighs, "Let's go." She is carried down to
the water and placed in the forward part of the boat.

The kid has been taking all this in on the edge of the cliff. I
go over and ask, "You ready to go?"

"I am not going back in that boat. This river sucks. Point
me towards the road. I am walking out."

"You can't walk out. You don't have any shoes."

"I have these." She indicates the wet-suit boots.

"Those neoprene things. You will walk through those the
first mile. They are made for water, not rocks. She said there is no
trail. This is rough country as soon as your feet start to bleed and
blister, it will be dark. There is no phone, no food, and no fun.
Not to mention the snakes and the alligators waiting to get you."

"There are no alligators out there." She is on to me. "And
Uncle Joe says you can hear the snakes coming. It is so dry they
carry canteens."

I counter with, "Well, I listened to your uncle Joe once
today." Meaning he was responsible for this adventure.

Daughter Dearest looks over the edge and finds her uncle
with her eyes and says, "Right, remind me to strangle him the first
chance I get."

I reason with her saying, "The quickest way out of here is
down the river. The only way out of here is down the river. They
are getting ready to go and we are burning daylight."

"They can go without me. I am walking."

"You will be safer with us. We are all going. Please come
with us. Look, everything the river can do to you, it has done.
You know exactly what to do. When you hit that water I was glad
you spend your summers taking swimming lessons. You know
how to swim. There won't be anything new. Keep your eye on
your guide. Do what Morgan tells you."

"If I get back in that boat, somebody is going to have to buy me something."

"Okay Baby, anything you want. Let's just try and get down this river without losing anybody. Remember we are all in the same boat."

We are the last ones in. The women are in the front. The men are in back. As we pull away I call, "You have more fun with Morgan." I had hoped to bolster the guide's courage. The crowd laughs, happy to be moving. We swiftly find what all the noise is about. The next hour is the longest five minutes of our lives. It is rough and wet, cold and death defying. Not the sort of thing to undertake unless you absolutely have to. The boat is up. The boat is down. The boat is spinning around. The boat is falling. The boat is flooding.

Morgan works his butt off keeping us in the safest part of the river. He rides it well. When we high side he doesn't get a word out before we are there, whichever shoulder he leans, to indicate direction, we do a human pyramid on. We exhibit the teamwork of a well-trained circus act. This boat will not go over again. The kid tells me later her right arm was getting blue from the water splashing it. Her left arm was turning blue from Aunt Carol's death grip on it.

Daughter Dearest asks Morgan, "Why do you go backwards over these rapids?"

He takes a measured breath and responds, "It is the only way I can control the boat. I don't have enough strength going forwards with this much weight."

"You're doing a fine job," says the kid.

Three mountain sheep are standing on the river's edge. As we whiz by, Morgan says, "Look, sheep."

The kid looks, and tells him, "Swell. Get me the hell out of here."

When we think it will never end, the boat snaps around a bend, and there is the blue bus. It is backed in the mud with the trailer in the water. Line handlers are in the shallows. They catch the boats as they come into view. We are beached and unloaded. Two of us hold Carol upright and another pumps her calves as we walk her through the mud and up to the bus.

On the ride back to town Carol is the center of attention. The chick in charge is still taking notes and thinking lawsuit. We are retelling the story and I ask Morgan, "How old are you anyway?"

The chick in charge holds up his scrawny arm and declares, "In one month he will be 18."

Always one to put people at ease I say, "Wow in one month you will be old enough to do this legally."

The chick in charge recovers, saying, "Tradition has it the guide whose boat goes over pays for the party."

Someone on the bus yells, "Are we all invited to the party?"

The boss says, "No, it is employees only." There is a collective moan and then laughter. We visit on the way back, leave our suits on the rack, and buy T-shirts that say, "I Survived Brown's Canyon." On the way out I press some bills into Morgan's hand and sincerely whisper, "Thank you for saving my family."

We take Carol home. She has a hot bath; two pain pills and goes to bed. We leave the kids with Grandma, and drive to Cripple Creek to gamble. We sit in the casino, drink whisky, and lose money. Perhaps we had used our luck for the day.

The kid has nightmares and won't cross that river on a bridge.

The biggest change is Carol. She saw the elephant under that boat and realized she has only one life. She took off to Kansas, married an Indian, and is having a good time. He rides bulls. She drives him to the rodeos.

MISS TIT SHOW

How do you make five pounds of fat look good? Put a nipple on it.

Miss Tit Show went to school with us. We were good friends. Everything she had was big. She went bra-less year after year, and those things rolling around in her sweater drove us crazy. We likened her to a moped. Fun while you are on it, but you don't want your friends to see you. Ms. Show reminded Lefty and me of the hostess at the dinner party.

She had large breasts. A drunk kept following her around trying to look down her shirt. She cornered him and snarled, "Hey buddy, what's with you?"

He slurred, "Lady, you got the greatest knockers. I will pay you $1500 just to kiss them." She was embarrassed and insulted and told her husband.

The husband said, "Not so fast Honey, we can use the money. Where is this guy?"

She pointed him out. They walked over. "Okay, you got a deal!" They went into a bedroom and she whipped off her top. The drunk grabbed one in each hand and moaned, he stuck his head right between them and used them for ear warmers. "Hurry up and kiss them," demanded the husband.

He pulled his head out, smiled and said, "I'd like to, but I just can't afford it."

I see a lot of silicone bouncing around. The plastic surgeons on vacation comment on it and watch it go by. They admire the scar-less techniques of someone else's work.

The older one from Alabama says, "That's my work. Those boobs are mine." or "I did her. That facelift is my work." He has the softest, steadiest hands. He doesn't drink alcohol. He sees what it does to his customers. He has Diet Coke and half a tuna sandwich, and talks to me in that soft southern drawl.

He assisted with the development of the techniques used today on the first breast implants in Houston. "Son, I make $6000 taking out a gall bladder or $20,000 doing a facelift. What do you think I'm going to do?"

His gift is counseling. Guys come in with their blond wives and want bonus knockers, the biggest they can get, handfuls of flesh, and he talks them out of it. "Hell man," he says. "You're going to kill her back making her carry those things around. She will be disfigured, and they will always be in her way. Give the little lady a break. Try something proportional that's bigger, but natural." Sometimes it works, sometimes it doesn't.

His work is art. He can make you gorgeous. He is the secret to eternal youth. It is amazing what money can buy. You wrap it in a designer thong and let it tag along, and it is a sign of success.

Day after day, behind the bar on the beach, with bronze goddesses just out of reach. "How do you take it?" asks a man. "Seeing this all the time."

I say for every blonde bombshell on the beach there is some guy somewhere who can't stand the sight of her. A woman is the only hunter that uses herself as bait. Why do women use makeup and perfume? They are ugly, and they smell bad.

When all the beaches are lined with peaches, what are the two things men never tire of watching? Fire and falling water. What is the difference between a golf ball and a g-spot? A guy will spend all day looking for a golf ball.

I've worked with guys who had a hard time with it. We lost a beach boy because he couldn't con a rich lady into adopting him. He gave her offers she could refuse. Beautiful women make men lose their heads. Men give up their wives, kids, families, jobs, relationships, careers, kingdoms, habits, opportunities and commitments for the spark of what is missing. Sometimes it works, sometimes it doesn't.

You only go around once, and it's really what makes you happy that counts. But, if you are thinking about doing this, my advice is--don't.

There is a busy bar on the promenade level, between the dining rooms. All the action is there. The people checking in and out share their alohas on the slate floors quarried in Mexico. There is a sea of marble-topped tables, separated by white pillars holding mahogany-covered ceilings. Three elderly women sat in the chairs with their backs to the rock wall. They were looking out at the ocean and over the walkway up from the beach. They had just lamented about how they always came with their husbands in the past. But this year they all were divorced so they came by themselves.

Suddenly three old men, with three young ladies, came walking up the ramp. One by one the women said, "That looks like my George."

"That is Fred."

"Oh, no it's Harry." They stood, threw some cash on the bar, walked up the stairs to the lobby, checked out and were gone. They didn't see each other.

Love is grand. Divorce is a hundred grand.

Be careful whom you marry in this life.

There was an old man who hired a young lady to be his secretary. She passed the wall test. He had all the applicants walk into the wall. If their nose touched first, they didn't get the job.

They worked well together, and became good friends. Then they started having an affair. One day she said, "We ought to get married."

"No," he said. "I am old enough to be your father. In a few years I am not going to be able to have sex the way you like it. You will want a much younger man."

So, the affair continues, and one day she reads about an operation in Sweden where the end of an elephant's trunk is grafted onto the male member. She says, "We should go check this out." They do and she convinces him to have this surgery. After three weeks of being black and blue the sex is better than ever. Then he wants to get married. So they have a big wedding and reception over at the mother-in-law's house.

After dinner, the old guy pushes himself back from the table and undoes the top button on his pants. As he is getting comfortable, the elephant's trunk comes out and grabs a baked potato off the table and disappears. Everybody sees it, but nobody says a word. Finally the mother-in-law breaks the ice and says, "I saw that. Did you see that? Hey, can you do that again?"

"I don't know. First time I have ever done it. But, I don't think my butt can take another baked potato."

I see a lot of guys on their second wives. They do a lot to keep them happy. What goes around gets dizzy and falls over. It is a way of staying young, if you can keep up. One of them told me his new, young wife wanted sex five nights a week. Just because she was marrying him, she didn't plan to give up any sex. He said, "Fine, put me down for Monday and Friday."

Four old guys were at the bar. One of them had just married a young girl and was being ribbed by the others. "Is she pretty?" they asked.

"No."

"Can she cook?"

"No."

"Is she rich?"

"No, she doesn't have any money."

"Why did you marry her?" they quizzed.

"Because, she can drive at night," he replied.

Sometimes I feel like a 20-year-old, but there is never one available.

These things can also go full circle. A young girl marries an old man. He divorces his wife, who gets the bulk of the estate. The old man dies. The girl inherits a little bit. She then marries someone her age that is successful. After 30 years and three kids the cycle repeats. He divorces her for the new Miss Tit Show and she gets the bulk of the estate, and a share in the blues she caused when she was younger.

MARCOS

Any institution that employs 800 people is bound to have petty jealousies, real hatreds and love affairs. Love is a long and slender thing. A mentor, in the beginning, told me, "Don't mess with the women where you work, unless you are in a position to hire and fire them." I messed with a woman at work one time, and am still married to her. Love is blind; marriage is a real eye-opener. At some workplaces women surround. In hospitals it's nurses; at newspapers it's secretaries, and at resorts they run the place.

Marcos was working the beach bar when I washed in from a shipwreck. She was the Filipino Goddess of Love. She had the flat Filipino nose, the flat Filipino chest, just under five-feet tall and maybe 75-pounds. She was what men call a "spinner." You balance her on your erection, slap her on the ass and she spins and giggles. Good fun. She had the most beautiful skin, ivory teeth, and perfect black hair. She was a seductress extraordinaire.

The bar was small, round, and had 10 chairs. There was one station and it was fast. A few steps away was a sandwich shop. We were in the back closing, the day I met her. "So this is where they make sandwiches?"

She said, "Yes," and closed the door. Then she pulled down her pants and leaned over a low cabinet and asked, "Why don't you show me what you can do with your hot-dog?"

I looked at that steaming beaver and thought, this one has been around. I said, "No thanks. I just put one out. I've been trying to give them up." She stood up, buttoned up and left, looking at me like I was strange. I realized why some of the guys had lipstick on their flies.

Any woman who will have sex with me at the first meeting probably screws every man she meets. She may be carrying something I don't want to take home to Mamma. In the Hospital Corps I saw a lot of venereal disease. Some you can cure, some you can't. A sailor would come in with a dose. We would treat him and do follow-ups with the Health Department to treat her. Women can carry something and not know it.

Marcos was in bed with the managers. She always got her way. She was in bed with some other bartenders. She was in bed with the union guys and the security guards. Hotel managers came from mainland hotels, often without their wife and kids. They stayed in the hotel, sometimes for months, until they could arrange living quarters and fly in their family. Marcos would be waiting in their room to welcome them after a long day. She knew how to impress a man, be naked and bring beer.

After a few years, the resort replaced the beach bar with a new one. This one was a decagon with 20 chairs and two stations. Now one bartender opened and worked until Marcos came in. It was a short shift, but it was a day job. I took it and worked with her five days a week. It was cool. I started learning the people's names and bouncing my one-liners off them. I was doing pretty well at making drinks and tips. Word got around that I was funny; just be careful what you ask him.

When Marcos walked in and I was getting ready to leave, she demanded half of my tips for my shift. I told her she was crazy, and she went to management. They came back and said it was her bar, and do it her way. One even confided in me that he knew it wasn't fair, but he was caught between a "rock and a hard place by Marcos."

The cash tips went in my pocket. They were minimal. It was a private bar for hotel guests only. With everybody wearing a swimming suit and a gold chain, who has cash? The tips were charged to the rooms and then divided by the cashier. I went to management and demanded half her tips from her shift. They thought I was crazy. "You're not even there for her shift," they explained to me.

"She's not even there for my shift either." I yelled at the highest mountain. It fell on deaf ears. The union wouldn't help. I hate being extorted. More than once I mulled over moving on, but that would have only made her happy. Making Marcos happy wasn't on my list of things to do.

I was getting screwed and not kissed. I began to hope I wouldn't get tipped so I wouldn't have to share. On days when it was busy and we worked together until dark, she still took half of my tips and kept all her own. A man will tip a pretty woman more money than a woman will ever tip a man. More men tip than women. She would have a glass full of 20's and 100-dollar bills. It all went in her purse.

Marcos demanded 10% of the cocktail waitresses' tips. Those kids were walking the sand in the sun. They were paid the minimum wage and depended on their tips to survive. Some of them were single parents. Hawaii is an expensive place to live. Bartenders are paid a living wage. They make $1 less an hour, than a chef. I told those girls, "You don't have to tip me, and don't tip Marcos either. She makes more than all of us." They stopped tipping. Marcos hated me for that.

She would be down there with her shirt unbuttoned to the waist, giving the old guys a taste. I would tell her, "Hey! Marcos, button up. You're scaring the horses." They would press a room key into her hand and she would whisper a time. After her shift as a bartender, she would take a shower and hit the halls as a whore. She could do five tricks by midnight and go home with an extra $500 in her jeans.

She had relatives: brothers, sisters or cousins in every department. She was a local girl and knew all the employees. She had a large, extended family that was spread on every island of the chain. If her father was sick in Honolulu, or an aunt on Maui, she had to go be with them. The papers went in, she was paid for the day, and the lay. The rumor was afoot and it was something for the department to believe. She ran her racket with impunity. Anyone who noticed was either in on it, and had a scam of their own, or kept their mouth shut because they were scared of her. She could get by with murder. She would come in late and leave early. If she wanted to abandon her bar and go upstairs to the Tear Ass and have a drink, nobody said anything.

She was off on weekends. She took time off during the week to carry on her affairs. If a man wanted to meet her on another island to play slap and tickle for the day, she went away. I was called back, on my day off, to work her shift. It didn't matter if I had a road trip planned with the Psycho Veterans' Motorcycle Club (We ride for those who aren't in there), or a sailboat race with Bill. I had to come in and cover.

If she drank too much alcohol the night before, or snorted too much cocaine that morning and couldn't come in, I took both shifts. It was a stretch, but it was the only way to keep all my tips.

If you see potential, stick around. She didn't abuse sick leave because any minute she was away from the bar she was losing money. She would only be away if someone else paid, and there was a bonus. She was a party animal. If she had no Johns waiting, then she was in the local bars hooking. Her favorite trick was to sit next to a dick, and swing her legs over his lap.

By way of conversation she explained the custom of wearing flowers in the hair. If a girl is available, it is over her right ear. If the woman is married, the flower is over her left ear. If she is married and available, then it is on top of the head. "What do Hawaiian women put behind their ears to attract men? Their feet!" She smiled and gave them a wink from an almond-sized eye. She was every sailor's dream come true.

There was no middle ground with her. Every man was either in love with her and lusting after her, or being blackmailed by her. If a lover was caught in the middle and didn't want to do things her way, all she had to say was, "How about I call your wife and tell her about the affair we're having?"

If he said, "I'll tell her it was a mistake. A short fling that's over."

"And, how about if I tell my husband?"

"I didn't know you were married. Who's your husband?"

Just the mention of his name would make them blanch. He was the biggest, blackest, ugliest Hawaiian on the island. At six-feet-five and 400 pounds, when he stood up the sun went down. He worked in engineering. While everyone else carried a belt full of tools, he carried a large hammer. That was also his name. He came from a family of bad-asses. They made the police report on Saturday night and the crime page Sunday morning. Hammer was a bad dude. What wasn't scar tissue was tattooed. He had a thing for white women and cruised for them in the parks.

He may or may not have known about the affair. He may or may not have cared. They had an open marriage. He was still married to the bitch, and if she said, "sic 'em" he would hit 'em. I gave him a wide berth. It was better to give Marcos what she wanted than to wake up dead in a cane field.

It went on like this for years, until we started getting gay managers. There were three, pretty boys who were flashy dressers and only interested in each other. Marcos couldn't seduce them.

Then things began to change. The first thing to come up was the tip. I refused to give her any more money. She went and raised hell with the gays. They had a deaf ear and a blind eye. They decided any tips we made were ours and nobody else could tell us what to do with them. It was our money. If she didn't like it, she could head down the road to where she would be happy. If you got a tip you shoved it in your pocket. If anybody asked, you said, "What tip?"

It was noticed that she didn't go home after work. It was against the house rules to be on property without a pass, if you aren't on the schedule. They had a female security guard escort her to her car after her shift.

Then they fired Hammer. Without him around to intimidate everybody, Marcos lost a lot of power. She quit and went down the road to a new resort being opened. She was in on the ground floor, and took her business with her. Some guys like dealing with an established firm.

I see her driving by in her new Corvette. There is a bra on the front of it. She should own at least one. She keeps Hammer in monster trucks. Big woman big pussy, little woman all pussy. Marcos makes it pay.

ORDER INFORMATION

Telephone orders: Call **(808) 889-6716**
Please have your credit card ready.

Please Use the Order Form on the next page.

Fax orders to   **(808) 889-1037**

Mail orders to   Allen Publishing
                            P.O. Box 479
                            Kapaau, HI 96755 USA.

For more information E-mail **jung@ilhawaii.net**

ORDER FORM Fax or Mail

Name_____

Address_____

City_____State_____Zip_____-_____

Telephone_____E-mail_____

Please send_____ copies of MY LIFE BEHIND BARS, by Jim Jung.

Hardcover $27.95 Paperback $19.95   Subtotal _____

Shipping – See Below   _____

Sales Tax – If shipped to Hawaii add 4%   _____

                              Total   _____

Payment: Check_____Credit Card_____

                Card Type_____

Card number_____

Name on card_____Exp. date_____ / _____

Signature_____
Shipping: US: $5.00 first book & $3.00 for each additional book.
International: $10.00 First book & $6.00 for each additional book.
Prices subject to change without notice.

ORDER INFORMATION

Telephone orders: Call **(808) 889-6716**
Please have your credit card ready.

Please Use the Order Form on the next page.

Fax orders to   **(808) 889-1037**

Mail orders to   Allen Publishing
                             P.O. Box 479
                             Kapaau, HI 96755 USA.

For more information E-mail **jung@ilhawaii.net**